SIMPLY

GOOD NEWS

SIMPLY

GOOD NEWS

Why the Gospel Is News
and What Makes It Good

N. T. WRIGHT

HarperOne
An Imprint of HarperCollins*Publishers*

HarperOne

FIRST EDITION

Library of Congress Cataloging-in-Publication Data

Wright, N. T. (Nicholas Thomas)
  Simply good news : why the gospel is news and what makes it good / N.T.
Wright.—First edition.
      pages cm
  ISBN 978–0–06–233434–3 (hardcover)
  ISBN 978–0–06–233435–0 (paperback)
  1. Apologetics. I. Title.
  BT1103.W75 2015
  230—DC23

                                    2014028420

  16 17 18 19   RRD(H)   10 9 8 7 6 5 4

For

David and Karen Seemuth

and

Guy and Katie Thomas

CONTENTS

SIMPLY

GOOD NEWS

Premise of book is it correct?

Who came first Paul or Jesus?
What is considered the World?

I

———

What's the News?

YOU ARE SITTING quietly in a café with a couple of
friends when suddenly the door bursts open and in
rushes a stranger with a wild, excited look on his face.

"Good news!" he shouts. "You'll never guess! The greatest
news you can imagine!"

What on earth can he be talking about? What could his *good
news* be, and why does he think it justifies barging into a café and
telling strangers about it?

Scenario 1: Perhaps the doctors just told him they had man-
aged to cure his daughter of the disease that was killing her. That
would be great news indeed, at least for his immediate family
and friends, but it does not explain why he would announce it to
strangers.

Scenario 2: Perhaps he heard that the local football team had
won a great victory against their old rivals down the road. In
some parts of my own country, people would indeed celebrate

such a thing as good news, though most fans probably would have been at the pub watching the game with him. Why leave the celebration to tell the nonfans at the café?

Scenario 3: Perhaps, in a region with high unemployment and poverty, he just learned that people had discovered huge new reserves of coal, oil, or gas. Suddenly there would be thousands of new jobs and a new start for everyone. I know places where that would cause otherwise quiet people to burst into a room and shout the news to everybody. That might justify such a dramatic announcement.

I start with these scenarios because I think we have lost touch with a basic element of the Christian faith. The Christian faith, in its earliest forms, is presented as *good news.* That is the original meaning of the Old English word *gospel.* I am arguing that the idea of seeing the Christian faith as *news* that is *good* is itself, ironically, news to many people today. Even those who know in theory that this is what *gospel* means often fail to appreciate the significance of the fact. We need, I suggest, to ask afresh: What is the good news that Jesus himself announced and told his followers to announce as well?

Most people—including many Christians—never ask themselves this question. We assume we understand the gospel because it seems so familiar and so entrenched. So we skip over the significance of why Christianity comes to us in the form of an announcement of the best possible news. The word *gospel* now carries different meanings. We talk of "gospel truth" when we want to stress how *reliable* something is. In some churches, "preaching the gospel" means explaining how to become a Christian—a formula we use to make sure we arrive in heaven safe and sound. For others, "gospel" is simply a type of music—though, granted, gospel music does often give the impression that something exciting is happening.

But when Jesus and the early Christians spoke of good news—which they did a great deal—they meant much more than this. They really did see it as news, and they believed this news was so good that it was worth announcing as widely as possible. Many churches and many Christian preachers and teachers manage to ignore this. Usually people outside the Christian faith don't realize that this is what Christianity is supposed to be about.

Let's go back to the stranger in the café. Each of the options I suggested has a particular shape that helps us understand more deeply what is meant by *good news*.

First, the news in each case isn't just something that has happened out of the blue. Each one of the announcements I mentioned assumes a larger context, as if it were *a new and unexpected development* within *a much longer story*. In the first case, the announcement comes amid the story of a sick and dying child. In the second, the longer running story is that of the well-known sporting rivalry between the teams. In the third case, the announcement comes in the context of the slow, sickening decline of a whole region into social deprivation. The news in question makes sense *within that longer story*. Only by knowing this backstory can we understand why the new announcement is good news.

Second, this news is about something that *has* happened, because of which *everything will now be different.* This news has significance; it makes an impact—it has consequences that alter lives. When you put good news within the longer story, it isn't just a matter of "well, that was nice, but now we go back to how things were before." (In the case of the football victory, it might feel like that after a few weeks, but at the time it always registers as a new beginning.) The child is going to get better! The whole region is going to recover! Life has been transformed!

Third, the news introduces *an intermediate period of waiting.* The child is still in the hospital—but instead of waiting anxiously and sorrowfully, we are now waiting with excitement and joy for her to get better and come home. Half the workforce is still unemployed, but now they will lift their aspirations and look forward to healthy activity and the resulting prosperity.

What good news regularly does, then, is to put a new event into an old story, point to a wonderful future hitherto out of reach, and so introduce a new period in which, instead of living a hopeless life, people are now waiting with excitement for what they know is on the way.

The Christian good news is supposed to be this kind of thing. The gospel of Jesus Christ comes as news within a larger story. It points to a wonderful new future. And it introduces a new period of waiting that changes our expectations. I am writing this book because I think many people, inside the church as well as outside, have seldom heard the gospel story told in this fashion. As a result, all sorts of things get muddled.

Good Advice, Wrong News

In many churches, the good *news* has subtly changed into good *advice*: Here's how to live, they say. Here's how to pray. Here are techniques for helping you become a better Christian, a better person, a better wife or husband. And in particular, here's how to make sure you're on the right track for what happens after death. Take this advice: say this prayer and you'll be saved. You won't go to hell; you'll go to heaven. Here's how to do it. *NO*

This is *advice,* not *news.*

The whole point of advice is to make you do something to get a desired result. Now, there's nothing wrong with good advice. We all need it. But it isn't the same thing as news. News is an announcement that something significant has happened. And good news is what Jesus and his first followers were all about.

At this point someone will object, "My church hasn't forgotten the good news! We know that Jesus died for our sins! He took our punishment so that we could go to heaven! Isn't that good news? If you thought you were destined for hell and suddenly someone told you God had done something about it, wouldn't that be good news?"

Well, yes, it would. But—and this is the shocking and difficult thing for many people—*that isn't exactly the good news Jesus and the early church were talking about.*

In other words, while some Christian teachers have exchanged good news for good advice, others have preserved the gospel as news, but they are telling a different story from what the New Testament authors meant by *good news.*

Yes, the good news is indeed about Jesus, and about his death and resurrection in particular. Yes, this good news does indeed open up a vision of an ultimate future beyond death, so that we live in hope and joy meanwhile. But the usual heaven-and-hell scheme, however popular, distorts the Bible's good news. Over many centuries, Western churches have got the story wrong. They have forgotten what the backstory is (the larger story that gives meaning and context to the good news). As a result, the news that bursts in upon it means something significantly different, and the long-range vista opened up by this news means something different again.

This affects everything: how we understand our relationship to God, our future, our responsibilities as a church and as disciples, and much more.

My main point, then, is that the Christian message is about good news, not good advice. And one of the reasons we need to sort this out is that many people have lived with a distorted version of the good news.

Let me sharpen this with two memories, one very recent, the other from some years ago.

I received an e-mail the other day from a man I have never met (a frequent enough occurrence). He had read one of my books, though—or at least part of it. He had seen enough to make him want to confront me with a question that, I suspect, bothers a lot of people. He wrote, "For a start, the Christian faith isn't 'news.' It's two thousand years old. And we've learned a lot since then. For another thing, when I hear you people talk about it, I don't think it's very 'good.' All that stuff about a distant deity threatening us with hellfire and damnation and then—if you're lucky—offering you a sneaky way out around the back. Calling it 'good news' seems a bit of a con, to put it mildly."

Those are excellent questions. Indeed, how can something that happened two thousand years ago still be considered news, and why are we so convinced that it deserves the adjective *good*? As I mentioned above, good news can only be understood in the context of a larger or earlier story. And if the gospel's backstory is that we're all going to hell unless a new way opens up, then that message often comes across not in terms of news (an announcement of something that has happened) but in terms of advice (guidance on what we must do). The good advice sounds like this: "There is a heaven, and there is a hell, so if I were you I'd grab my chance to make the right choice." If there is any news there—perhaps the suggestion that Jesus offers a way of making that choice successfully—then my correspondent would be right: that is quite old news, and it is only good for the lucky ones who heed the advice.

The problem with explaining the gospel this way is that Jesus himself didn't actually say much about heaven in the sense we normally mean it. When he spoke of heaven's kingdom, he wasn't talking about a place called heaven to which people might or might not go after they die. He was talking about something that would become a reality "as in heaven, so on earth" (Matt. 6:10).

Difference between God + heaven?

heaven

God only coming to
Earth - not every where
? is universe.

So instead of suggesting that we could escape the earth to go to heaven, Jesus's good news was about heaven coming to earth. And there are many people inside and outside the church who have never heard this news. It isn't only the atheists who have got hold of the wrong end of the stick.

My other memory will serve as a parable that illustrates the problem with good news. Jesus and the early Christians faced this problem, and so do we.

On November 22, 2003, I woke up very early and immediately telephoned my daughter. She was at home in England; I was in a hotel in Atlanta, Georgia, attending the annual meeting of the Society of Biblical Literature. But the reason for my call was in Australia, where the English Rugby Union team was playing in the final of the game's biggest challenge: the Rugby World Cup. Their opponent in the final was the host nation, Australia. That country, always crazy about sport—especially against England!— was on tiptoe with excitement, urging their team to victory. I had been following the contest through all the preliminary rounds. As England won game after game, getting through the early stages and then into the final, hope had been building. Could they make it all the way? Might it really be possible? I wanted to hear the news. Actually, *wanted* is far too weak a word. I was eager for it. Hungry.

The reason I phoned my daughter was that, though the television in my hotel room offered hundreds of channels, I couldn't find the game on any of them. Rugby, it seemed, hadn't made it onto the American radar. I knew, however, that my daughter would be glued to the relevant English television station. With a quiver in her voice, she told me the news: The game had reached full time, with the two sides exactly even at seventeen points each. Half an hour of extra time was being added. The players, having given their all, would now have to find yet more reserves of energy and determination. The atmosphere was electric. It was unbearably tense. This was as big as a sporting contest could get.

There was no question of going back to sleep. I got dressed and went down to the hotel lobby, where all was quiet, it being around five in the morning. Half an hour later I telephoned again. My daughter was shouting with joy. Jonny Wilkinson, the poster boy of English rugby, had won the game with a drop-goal in the final half minute. Australia was devastated; England was ecstatic. *I* was ecstatic. This was the best sporting news England had had for many a long day. If part of the definition of *good news* might be "something you want to shout across the street," this certainly fell in that category. Americans often encourage one another to think positively, whatever the circumstances. But I didn't need any encouragement that morning. Something had *happened* that made all the difference.

The trouble was, who could I tell? Who wanted to hear this good news? It was still early morning in Atlanta. I wanted to go to the reception desk in excitement and tell the clerks, "We just won the cup!" I wanted to hug the concierge and say, "Did you hear the news?" I wanted to shout it out to the sleepy joggers setting off on their morning run. I wanted to put up a big notice for everyone to see: "ENGLAND WON THE WORLD CUP!" I thought of trying to tell the night porters who were hanging around.

But I knew it was no good. None of the hotel staff was remotely likely to be interested. They didn't even know who Jonny Wilkinson was. American football has recently become big news in England, but its transatlantic cousin hadn't yet hit the headlines in America. What was good news for me, and for my whole country, wouldn't register in the hotel lobby at 5 A.M. I might as well go out into the street in a Scottish town and announce that China had beaten Germany in the World Table Tennis Championships. All I would get is a shrug of the shoulders and a big yawn: "So what?"

Then the crowning irony. As the day dawned and the confer-ence woke up, I went to join the line for breakfast. I was looking for someone, anyone, who even knew that a major sporting event had taken place—someone to whom I could tell my good news. And the first person I met who knew about the game was . . . an Australian. He, of course, was crestfallen. What was good news for me was bad news for him. The message about the World Cup was foolish to Americans and scandalous to Australians. But it kept me happy all week. And—this is the point of what news does—in bringing one story to its explosive climax, it opened up another one. English rugby entered a new era. Lots of little boys suddenly wanted to be Jonny Wilkinson when they grew up.

Sports provide us with dangerous metaphors. A sporting con-test is a *contest*: a game of winners and losers. We love it when our team wins, and we hate it when they lose. The good news about Jesus isn't supposed to be like that, though that's the impression people often get. We will explore this further in due course. But for an English rugby fan in 2003, this announcement was most definitely good news.

Roman Good News

Let me turn now to another illustration. This one comes from the time and place where Jesus himself burst on the scene with his original good news, where Saint Paul went with the gospel: the world of the early Roman Empire. Come back with me to the first century, to the rise and accession of the man who became the first real Roman emperor, the man under whose reign Jesus of Nazareth was born.

Julius Caesar, perhaps the best-known Roman of all, was never officially emperor. The reason he was assassinated in March of 44 BC was precisely because his enemies didn't want anybody to become the sole ruler. But, as often happens, political violence plunged their world into turmoil and civil war. Rome had become great through relentless and ruthless military conquest. Now all that expertise was turned inward.

The civil war focused initially on the struggle between those who had killed Julius Caesar and those who wanted to avenge his death. For this purpose, Caesar's adopted son and heir, the young Octavian, teamed up with Mark Antony, who had been Caesar's friend. Shakespeare's plays about Julius Caesar and Antony and Cleopatra have ensured that many people who have never studied ancient history are nonetheless able to imagine all this going on.

But the alliance was short lived. Once Caesar's assassins, Brutus and Cassius, had been defeated, Antony and Octavian became rivals for ultimate power. Antony traveled around what we now call the Middle East, drumming up massive support. But Octavian, though less experienced, was not going to give up without a struggle. The crucial battle took place at sea, on September 2nd of 31 BC, off the coast of Actium in western Greece. Octavian's navy won. Antony fled to Egypt with his famous consort, Cleopatra, where they both committed suicide.

Now, suppose you'd been living in Rome during this period— during thirteen years of civil war. It was a terrible time. Even though the fighting was taking place a long way off, the city itself would be full of rumors, factions, threats, and political jockeying for position. Everyone would be waiting anxiously for news from the front. Suppose you had been a friend of the Caesar family—a friend of the late Julius, and also of his heir Octavian. If Octavian won, it would be good news for you; if Antony won, it would be bad news for you (and you might have to leave town in a hurry).

Then, at last, Rome hears what has happened: "Good news! Octavian Caesar has won a great victory! He is now master of the whole Roman world!" This is good news about *something that has just happened.* The backstory of the civil war has come to a close. Peace is at hand. The word *good news* became a regular slogan for announcing to the world that Octavian, soon to be acclaimed as Augustus, by which he is now more usually known, had brought peace, justice, and prosperity to the world.

But it would immediately imply good news for you about *something that would shortly happen.* Octavian, having won the victory, would be coming back to Rome. First he would have to consolidate his victory, especially in Egypt, which was to become a vital part of the empire. There would be military mopping-up operations to make sure the victory was fully implemented. It would be nearly two years before Octavian finally returned to the capital, where he proclaimed that he had brought peace to the whole world. During those two years, the city was poised between the news about something that *had* just happened—his decisive victory—and the expectation of something that *would soon* happen, namely his return in triumph. That is what news does: it creates a new period of time.

During that time, people in Rome would know what was coming. Octavian would, of course, handsomely reward his friends and supporters. He would likely punish those who had supported Antony—not to mention those who had sided with Julius Caesar's assassins in the first place. For the moment, though, the city would be living *between the event that had just happened and the event that would shortly happen.* So, if we suppose you were a supporter of Augustus, the good news about the recent event and the good news about the imminent event would translate into good news about your life right now. Everything would look different. You and your family would prepare to celebrate. You would start to plan a whole new life. The world was going to change completely. Indeed, because of the recent victory, there would be a sense in which it was already a different place. And your life, right now, would be different as a result. Something *has* happened;

something therefore *will* happen. And *the way things are right now is different as a result.*

This is a perfect historical example of the way this type of good news worked in Jesus's and Paul's day—and how it still works today. When you think about how actual events occur in the real world, it becomes quite straightforward.

Now suppose you had been on the other side. Suppose you had secretly supported the assassination of Julius Caesar. Or suppose you had wanted Antony to win in the final showdown. I suggested a moment ago that this news might mean it was time for you to leave town in a hurry. But there was an alternative. Herod the Great, a powerful warlord in the Jewish homeland, had been made king of the Jews by the Roman authorities. He, like much of the Middle East, had supported Antony. He was now on the wrong side. But Herod was both bold and clever. He went straight to Octavian. Don't think, he said, about *whose* friend I have been. Think of *how loyal* a friend I have been. That's what I will be to you. Octavian, no stranger to realpolitik, reaffirmed Herod's place as king of the Jews. For Herod, the news of what *had* happened, and what it meant in terms of what *would* shortly happen, created a challenge to which he responded by casting himself on the mercy of the one who would now become king. It worked. Good news creates a new situation and calls for new decisions.

This example from the ancient Roman world is not, of course, selected at random. It isn't just an odd fragment of ancient history that merely happens to carry the same triple pattern—something that happened, something that will happen, a radical change in how things are right now as a result. Starting with Octavian, the Roman emperors regularly used the words *good news* to describe *both* what they had already achieved *and* what life would now be like as a consequence. When the early Christians used this language, they used it in a similar way. Something *had happened* because of which everything was now different. Something *would happen* that would complete this initial victory (like Octavian returning to Rome and setting up his court). As a result, *the present moment was new and different.* This good news transformed people's lives. It was bound to.

The story of Octavian, Antony, and Herod reminds us of something else. When Jesus was born, Augustus ruled much of the known world, and Herod ruled the Middle East. Jesus died under the reign of Augustus's successor, Tiberius, and under the local rule of one of Herod's sons, Antipas. Perhaps, for some people, this needs stressing. *Jesus of Nazareth was a real man, living and dying at a turbulent moment in real space-time history.* His message, and the message about him that the early Christians called good news, was not about how to escape that world. It was about how the one true God was changing it, radically and forever. *such a small period in time*

Come with me, then, back into that first-century Roman world, so that we can come to grips with what the Christian good news meant when it was first announced there. Let us find our way to a seaport in northern Greece, in the middle of the first century AD—a world by then quite familiar with the good news of the Roman Empire under Augustus and his successors. There, in this seaport, we come upon an odd, shabby, energetic little man announcing good news and watching as people's lives were transformed by it. Who was he, and what did he think he was up to?

had happened
↓
would happen
↓
present new + different

2

Foolish, Scandalous, or Good?

THE MAN WAS a Jew, born and bred in what is now southeastern Turkey. He was called Saul, a Hebrew name that, in his Jewish culture, had ancient royal associations. In Greek, however (Greek was the standard language around the Mediterranean world, like English is in many places today), the name Saul carried unpleasant overtones. It's as though somebody from a non-English culture had a name like Wimp or Slob and decided that in the English-speaking world he would change it to something less likely to evoke snickers. Saul changed his name to Paul.

I begin there because Paul must have realized early on that the good news he was called to announce would evoke quite enough snickering as it was. This has always been the case, and it is still the case today. That doesn't mean the good news is in fact incomprehensible, or meaningless, or stupid. But it will sound like that to some who hear it, which is what we should expect.

Paul believed he had a royal commission to announce the new good news to the world. The word he used for this commission, *apostle,* has become a dead metaphor in today's world, but for him it carried a special sense: commissioner. One who has been charged with a responsibility. One who is responsible to the king for carrying it out.

That king was, of course, Jesus.

So Paul found himself, after many early adventures, in the wealthy and thriving seaport of Thessalonica (modern Salonika or Thessaloniki). It was the capital of the region. He didn't spend long there, because his message and the effect it had on some people quickly made him unpopular.

When he wrote about the experience a few weeks later, in a letter to the small group of people whose lives had been transformed by his good news, he highlighted two things that most of his original audience in Thessalonica probably found odd—and offensive. He talked about a "different god." And he talked about someone called Jesus. We begin our exploration here because Paul's first letter to the Thessalonians is probably the earliest written record we have of the good news.

Despite Paul's talk about God, he was not telling people about a new religious system. Nor was he urging them to adopt a new type of morality. He wasn't offering them a new philosophy—a theory about the world, how it worked, how we could know things, how we should behave. Other teachers at the time were offering things like that, but Paul's approach was different. True, his message would eventually affect those areas, too. But many people today assume that Christianity is one or more of these things—a religion, a moral system, a philosophy. In other words, they assume that Christianity is about advice.

But it wasn't and isn't.

Christianity is, *simply, good news.* It is the news that *something has happened as a result of which the world is a different place.* That is what the apostle Paul—Paul the royal commissioner—was announcing.

To many people then, and to many today, this was and is either nonsense or offensive or both. One can debate the merits of a religion, moral system, or philosophy, but a news event is discussed in a different way. Either the event happened or it didn't; if it did happen, either it means what people say it means or it doesn't. So we begin to see the enormity of Paul's challenge. He is announcing that a world-changing event has happened, and he is announcing it to an audience composed of people who assume they would have heard of a world-changing event if one had really occurred. And they hadn't.

Paul himself pointed out in another letter that his message was "a scandal to Jews and folly to Gentiles" (1 Cor. 1:23), much like the rugby result that was foolishness to Americans and scandalous to Australians. What sort of event did Paul have in mind? We have seen that everybody in the Roman world knew a major military victory could change everything. Our world today is still shaped, in powerful ways, by Augustus's victory and the way he then organized the empire.

The Christian claim, remarkably, is that the world is a different place, in a different way, not because of Augustus but because of Jesus. Not because of great affairs of state in the first-century Roman world, but because of something that happened in a far-off province near the eastern frontier of the Roman Empire in the same period. The good news that Jesus announced, like the good news that his first followers announced *about* him, was not a piece of advice, however good. It was about something that *had* happened, about something that *would* happen as a result, and about the new moment between those two, the moment in which people were in fact living, whether they realized it or not.

As you might expect, the emphasis was always on what *had* happened. Everything else followed from that. Something had happened that changed everything, and Paul was announcing this message so that it would grasp people's hearts, minds, and imaginations and transform their lives.

We began this book with a man bursting into a café and announcing good news. Paul was like that. He believed that he knew something worth announcing to surprised strangers: "Good news! You'll never guess! The greatest news you can imagine!"

The King's Herald

So what was he talking about in Thessalonica and several other cities in the middle of the first century? In what sense was he bringing good news? What did he think had happened that made an all-important difference to the world?

Paul had several ways of summarizing his message. But in the letter he wrote to the church in Thessalonica, not long after his first visit there, he puts it like this. He describes what happened when he first announced the good news to them, taking his description, he says, from the reports he's heard from other communities. "They themselves tell the story," he says, "of the kind of welcome we had from you":

> You turned to God from idols, to serve a living and true God, and to wait for his son from heaven, whom he raised from the dead—Jesus, who delivers us from the coming fury. (1 Thess. 1:9–10)

That tells us about the focus of Paul's announcement. It was a message about Jesus, and consequently a message about a true God—as opposed to the many other gods that filled the culture of the ancient world. Something had happened to Jesus: he had been raised from the dead. This event had disclosed a previously unexpected reality: that all these other gods were a sham, mere

God wasn't new only new way of viewing God.

what had a new God vs idols and Jesus at same time coincidence?

idols, but there was one God who really deserved that name. And he was alive and active. Paul had many ways of saying all this, but however you approached it, this was the heart of his message: an event involving Jesus and a revelation of the one true God. Something that had made the world a whole different place. Something because of which people were now faced with a challenge (like Herod faced with Octavian's victory): If this is the new reality, where do you stand in relation to it?

We will say more about both elements of this good news in a little while. But it's important to emphasize right away that what Paul was talking about was not what most people today imagine. If you mention the Christian good news, most people today imagine that you're talking about *an option you might like to take up if you feel so inclined.* A piece of advice. For some, it's a *No* new kind of spirituality: here is a Jesus-focused interior life for those who want that kind of thing. For others, it's a new way of living: here is a Jesus-based morality you, or indeed your community, might like to follow. For others again, it's about taking out an option on your future—a kind of retirement plan, except that the retirement in question takes place after your death rather than before it. It's a way of making sure that you at least will be safe and sound, even if the rest of the world isn't. Some people, as we will see, highlight this last element, and when they talk about the good news or the gospel, they focus almost exclusively on this aspect. Some people do the same with the idea of reestablishing our present relationship with God after being cut off through sin.

None of these ways of looking at things are, as they stand, totally wrong. The message *of* Jesus and the message *about* Jesus do include something about spirituality, something about morality, something about the ultimate future, something not least about our relationship with God. But all these miss the main point. The good news brought by Paul (and before him, by

Paul by Jesus

Jesus, though we will come to that presently) was not about an option you might wish to take up. It wasn't a piece of *advice* about something you might or might not wish to do. *It was news.* They claimed it was *good news.*

When Paul told people his good news, he didn't mean for them to say, "Well, that's interesting. I'll see if that's going to suit me or not." He wasn't inviting them to try on a new way of thinking or living that would enable them to live differently or think differently. He was telling them that something had happened which had changed the world, that the world was now a different place, and that he was summoning them to be part of that new, different reality. He was telling them about an event that would cause them to adjust their entire lives in order to come into line with the way things now were.

Paul said

It isn't difficult to see how this worked. When Roman heralds came into a city like Thessalonica announcing that a new emperor had been enthroned, they didn't mean, "Here is a new sort of imperial experience, and you might like to see if it suits you." They meant, "Tiberius (or Claudius, or Nero, or whoever) is the Lord of the World. You are the lucky recipients of this good news; he demands your loyalty, your allegiance, and (of course) your taxes." That's how the Roman good news worked. The heralds might have said, "If you take my advice, you'll do what you're told," but this piece of *advice* meant what it meant because of the *news* about the new imperial fact that had been launched upon the world, whether the world wanted it or not.

When we change the details, we can see that this is also how Paul's good news worked. Paul used the word *herald* to talk about his own vocation of announcing the good news about Jesus (1 Tim. 2:7). He wasn't like someone offering people a new type of torch so they could see better in the dark. He was like someone saying that the sun had risen, and that if you would only open the curtains you'd see that you don't need torches anymore.

It was already there; now wake up and observe / partake.

Not That facts had change.

The Backstory

In particular, Paul was saying that they didn't need the old gods anymore. At this point he was presenting to the world an essentially Jewish message. The Jewish people cherished their ancient scriptures, in which, across many centuries, prophets, scribes, and wise thinkers of Israel had insisted that the gods of the nations were simply human artifacts, man-made fabrications, idols constructed of wood, stone, or precious metal. They possessed neither life nor power. By contrast, the God of Israel (so they claimed) was alive and active. Nor was he simply the God of Israel, a local or private deity. He was the creator, the God of the whole world.

All this might have been said by any devout Jew at any time in the ancient world. It might well, however, have been seen as fighting talk by non-Jewish hearers. Every city and region had its own divinities. Every human activity had gods or goddesses associated with it. The way you made sure life was working all right was to keep those divinities happy. To abandon them—to declare that they were lifeless nonentities and you weren't going to worship them anymore—would threaten to dissolve the glue that held society together. If you left off practicing the traditional forms of religion, especially sacrifices and festivals, bad things might happen—to the city, to the community, to your family, to you personally. If people refused to take part in the traditional observances, it was seen as scandalous, subversive, and revolutionary. If someone tried to introduce *new* gods into a community, that might be even worse (it did sometimes happen, but you had to be very careful). And if anyone said something had recently happened to *demonstrate* that the old gods were a sham, and that the new God was alive and active, this was likely to cause riots. Paul found that out the hard way.

To announce the Jewish God, then, would in principle be offensive and unwelcome. It would be like telling my Australian friend that England had won the cup. That, presumably, is why the Jewish people often remained in their own communities and didn't try to persuade non-Jews to give up their traditions and join them in worshipping the One God of Israel. The alternative to being offensive, then, was to be irrelevant: non-Jewish communities might know that some strange people lived in another part of town and didn't worship "the gods," but that was nothing to get excited about. It would be like me trying to tell the news of England's great victory to Americans. Paul's good news, which made such vital and vibrant sense to him, faced an early version of the challenge we face today, which I will discuss from various angles later on. This news is either offensive or boring. Either scandalous or merely nonsense.

The central Jewish belief—that though all other divinities were human artifacts, there really was one living and true God—might perhaps have been seen as good news. I can imagine an enthusiastic Jewish apologist presenting it as such to bored pagans, though we have no evidence that people were actually doing that ("Good news! There really is a living God!"). In any case, apart from the great foundational events of Israel's past, notably the exodus from Egypt fifteen hundred years earlier, nothing much had *happened* to create the sense that the world was now a different place, with the Jewish God in charge.

Paul, however, believed that something *had* now happened, as a result of which the ancient Israelite belief—that Israel's God was the creator of the whole world, and he was alive and active—had been dramatically vindicated. That was why Paul was not simply offering people advice about a new religion. He was offering good news about a different God. A living God. A God who had made himself known in and through Jesus of Nazareth.

This description of Paul's message and how it worked will

come as a surprise to many people in the modern Western world. There are two reasons for this. The first is that people often use the word *god* as if it always meant the same thing. But that's just the point: it doesn't. The second is that people often imagine the main purpose of Christianity to be getting people to heaven and teaching them to behave along the way—or perhaps, getting them to behave in such a way that they will get to heaven. That is a gross distortion.

One of the other Greek cities Paul visited was Corinth. In fact, he stayed there longer than most other places. Between visits, he wrote letters to the church there, covering a wide range of topics. In the first of those letters, he faced a number of questions and challenges. The final topic, which is a vital clue to most of the other things he has been writing about, is the resurrection.

To address this, he quotes what seems to be the standard early Christian summary of the good news. This is worth looking at carefully. Remember what we said earlier: for something to qualify as news, there has to be (1) an announcement of an event that has happened; (2) a larger context, a backstory, within which this makes sense; (3) a sudden unveiling of the new future that lies ahead; and (4) a transformation of the present moment, sitting between the event that *has* happened and the further event that therefore *will* happen. That is how news works. It is certainly how the early Christian good news worked:

> The Messiah died for our sins in accordance with the
> Bible; he was buried; he was raised on the third day in
> accordance with the Bible; he was seen by Cephas, then
> by the Twelve; then he was seen by over five hundred
> brothers and sisters at once, most of whom are still with
> us, though some fell asleep. (1 Cor. 15:3–6)

Paul goes on to talk of seeing the risen Jesus, but the bit I've quoted is the vital part as we try to understand his good news.

Everything pivots around the complex event that had happened: the Messiah died, was buried, was raised, was seen. Take that away and Christianity collapses. Put it in its proper place and the whole world is different. That is the news. (We will come back later to consider what exactly Jesus's resurrection meant and how we can answer sceptics who scoff at the very idea.)

Like the stranger rushing into the café, or like a sleepy Englishman in an American hotel wanting to tell people about England's victory over Australia, a great deal depends on the backstory. Unless you know what has happened earlier, you won't see the significance of the events. That was certainly so for Paul. That is why, twice within this little summary of the good news, Paul uses the phrase "in accordance with the Bible." What does that mean?

Paul's Bible was the Jewish Bible of the day, what Christians now call the Old Testament. Paul, like many Jews of the time, read this Bible as a single great story—but it was a story in search of an ending. It was about how God, who had created the world, called a single people, Israel, to be his people—but not for their own sake. He called them and made them special, so that through them he could rescue the world—the human race and the whole creation—from the appalling mess that had come about.

The trouble was, the people who were supposed to be carrying forward this divine rescue operation needed rescuing themselves. They shared in the same mess—the same rebellion against God, the same corruption and wickedness—as the rest of humankind. But their Bible still spoke of God doing a new thing, rescuing the rescuers, and getting the whole plan back on track. Some passages, including some famous ones, spoke of this happening through a coming king who would be "anointed" with God's own powerful Spirit in the way that monarchs were anointed with oil. By no means did all Jews in Paul's day believe in a coming anointed one. For those who did, this figure would embody the best news

annointed one

anyone had ever heard. He would rescue Israel, and with Israel all the human race, and with the human race all the world.

That is the backstory. That's what "according to the Bible" meant. And the word for "anointed" is *Messiah.* So when Paul says, "The Messiah died for our sins in accordance with the Bible," the news he is announcing means what it means within this ancient Jewish and biblical backstory. The one true God has done, at last, what Paul and others believed had to be done for the world to be at last put right.

(We need to pause at this point. Many people, including many Christians, assume a very different backstory. For some, it goes like this: What we need is life after death, but we're not sure if it's true or not. Now Jesus has been raised, so we know that there really is a life after death. For others, it goes like this: We aren't sure whether there is a God or not, or whether Jesus is divine— but he was raised from the dead, so there is a God, and Jesus is his son. For others again, there is a darker note: We believe in heaven and hell, but how can we know which direction we're heading? Answer: Jesus was raised, so all his people are going to heaven. There are numerous variations. Such notions are not one hundred percent wrong, but they are caricatures and, as such, highly misleading if embraced as if they were the real thing. Notice what they miss out. In all of these, the word *Messiah* [Christ] functions as a proper name. For Paul, it really means "Messiah." This goes closely with the true backstory for the good news: the Messiah died and was raised "in accordance with the Bible." In these caricatures, that would just mean, "We can find a few proof texts in the scriptures that prophesy resurrection." In Paul's mind, it means, "This is where God's plan to rescue the world through the call of Israel, and God's plan to rescue Israel itself to fulfill that original purpose, have finally been accomplished." The good news means what it means within the *original* backstory, not within the various low-grade caricatures that people sometimes embrace as if they were the real thing.)

So how does all this work out? The rest of the quite long chapter (1 Cor. 15) makes it clear—particularly verses 20–28. There Paul explains that, like Octavian/Augustus after his decisive victory over Antony, Jesus the Messiah is already ruling, but for the moment he has not completed the work of bringing everything, all rebel forces, under his authority:

God/Jesus?

> He has to go on ruling, you see, until "he has put all his enemies under his feet." Death is the last enemy to be destroyed. . . . [W]hen everything is put in order under him, then the son himself [Jesus] will be placed in proper order under the one who placed everything in order under him [God the Father], so that God may be all in all. (1 Cor. 15:25–28)

Don't understand.

God?

And Paul spells out in the rest of the chapter that what God did for Jesus at Easter, raising him from the dead, is what he will do for all his people in the end. Resurrection may be hard to imagine, in the first century or the twenty-first century, but Paul trains his readers to do just that. *The good news about what has happened points to the good news about what is yet to happen.* And those who find themselves grasped by this double good news also find that their lives between the one and the other are utterly transformed as a result.

Most of the rest of the letter is about exactly that. The problems Paul addresses—problems of personality cults in the church, problems of sexual morality, problems about how to live in the wider pagan world, problems about how to organize public worship—most of these problems relate more or less directly to the good news itself. Once people grasp that the events of the Messiah's death and resurrection have transformed everything and that they are now living between that initial explosive event and God's final setting right of the world (when God is "all in all"), then everything will change: belief, behavior, attitudes, expectations, and not least a new love, a real sense of belonging, which springs up among those who share all this. That is what so much of Paul's writing is about. Get the gospel right, and everything else will come right.

Foolishness, Scandals, and Power

But Paul knew perfectly well that getting the gospel right wasn't easy. As we have already hinted, there were huge pressures from two directions. Some thought it was all absolutely crazy. And some found it positively offensive. Remember how, when England won the rugby match, the news was completely uninteresting to the Americans, and the one Australian I met found it shameful? Here is Paul's equivalent. He knew that the good news came as a slap in the face to the two great ethnic groups in his world:

> In God's wisdom, the world didn't know God through
> wisdom, so it gave God pleasure, through the folly of
> our proclamation, to save those who believe. Jews look
> for signs, you see, and Greeks search for wisdom; but we
> announce the crucified Messiah, *a scandal to Jews and folly
> to Gentiles,* but to those who are called, Jews and Greeks
> alike, the Messiah—God's power and God's wisdom.
> God's folly is wiser than humans, you see, and God's
> weakness is stronger than humans. (1 Cor. 1:21–25,
> emphasis added)

This remarkable statement reflects something Paul discovered again and again. Think of what it was like. He arrives in a city, accompanied by one or two friends. He knows nobody there. Since he is a Jew, and he believes the good news is in accordance

If Jesus (Messiah) how could he welcome

with the Bible, the proper starting point is in the Jewish gathering places, but his message is shocking and usually unwelcome. A crucified Messiah? That's crazy. The Messiah is supposed to defeat Israel's enemies, not be killed by them. Crucifixion is shameful. It means God's curse is upon you. To suggest that such a person is God's chosen one, his anointed—well, it's a kind of blasphemy. Paul must have encountered that reaction again and again. All his careful explanations about how this was in fact what the Bible had predicted would be waved away—especially when some of the hearers realized he was also saying that this Messiah was going to welcome non-Jews (Gentiles or Greeks) just as much as Jews.

The reaction from his Jewish contemporaries was bad. But worse awaited him outside on the street. Paul's good news, his royal announcement about Jesus, was nonsense at every level. Think for a moment how it must have sounded.

Cities like Thessalonica, Philippi, or Corinth—all key centers of Paul's work—knew perfectly well what a royal announcement meant. "Good news—we have an emperor! He has saved the world! He has brought peace and justice to us all! He is our Lord! He is the son of God!" Now here is Paul saying, "Good news—the world has a new Lord! He is the true Son of God!" Already this sounds strange. Who is this odd little man, sounding as if he's a royal herald making a proclamation about a new emperor? And who is this new emperor, anyway?

Answer—he is a Jew! And he was crucified! He is called Jesus!

At this point mouths drop open with incredulity. People stare. Whoever this fellow Paul is, he must have been drinking something strange. Or sitting out in the sun for too long. Crucifixion is about the most shameful thing that can happen to you. And anyway it means he's dead. How can a crucified man be the Lord, the Son of God?

"No!" answers Paul. "He's alive! God raised him from the dead!"

Now the crowd is convinced Paul is mad. Everybody knows

perfectly well that dead people don't come back to life. Especially someone who has been crucified by those highly efficient killers, Roman soldiers.

But this is the heart of Paul's good news. *The Messiah died for our sins in accordance with the Bible . . . and he was raised on the third day in accordance with the Bible.* Understand the Bible and it all makes sense. But of course, being non-Jews, they don't know the Bible, still less understand it. And meanwhile the Jews who heard Paul in the synagogue are still alarmed. Is this going to mean a complete overhaul of their wonderful traditions, their whole way of life?

That's another question. But let's stick with what happens when Paul makes this announcement. He knows it makes no sense to his hearers. He knows that any Jews listening may well find it scandalous or even blasphemous. But he persists. There is after all one true God, the God of Israel. He made the whole world, and he planned an amazing rescue operation for that world. That's the backstory, and the news is that this rescue operation has now happened! Jesus, who died and was raised, is Israel's Messiah— and in Israel's Bible, the Messiah, when he comes, will be Lord of the whole world. That's why this is a message for everybody, not just Jews.

So what happens when Paul announces this message? This is where the truly strange bit happens. As we saw a moment ago, Paul says that the gospel is a scandal to Jews and folly to Gentiles (non-Jews), but "to those who are called" it will be "God's power and God's wisdom." What does he mean by "called"? And in what sense is this message "power and wisdom"?

Paul says similar things elsewhere, too. He declares in one passage that the good news is "God's power, bringing salvation" (Rom. 1:16). He speaks elsewhere about the gospel coming not "in word only, but in power, and in the holy spirit, and in great assurance" (1 Thess. 1:5). So what does all this mean?

[handwritten marginal notes: "what's world?" and "Energy made universe. So why true God only make earth."]

What Paul refers to is *something that happens when this good news is announced.* He had seen this happen again and again. Although this good news is a scandal to Jews; although this good news is crazy, stupid nonsense to non-Jews; although nobody in his or her right mind would believe it . . . yet, nevertheless, something happens to some of the people listening. The message, the royal announcement, seems to go into them like a hot drink on a cold day (perhaps, since we're talking about Greece, we might say a cold drink on a hot day). It refreshes them. It energizes them. Sometimes it even heals them of bodily ailments. They find, welling up inside, a sense of astonishment, of being loved. It's like what would happen to someone who had been profoundly deaf from birth and then, straight after a successful operation, heard the opening of a Mozart symphony. A whole new world, never before imagined, would open up. It's like what would happen to you if the person you loved best in all the world, and who you thought had been killed in a terrible accident, turned out to have been in a different car all along, and was alive and well and coming home within the hour.

With this comes a realization that, after all, this good news actually does make *sense.* Paul has seen this happen, too—seen what it's like when the light goes on in someone's face, when puzzlement or shock is suddenly replaced with a dawning recognition. He hasn't asked people to fit two or three awkward and incredible things into their existing view of the world; he has told them the most awkward and incredible thing you can imagine, in the sure knowledge that this news creates its own new world. But it isn't, as you might imagine, a world apart, a kind of zany private fantasyland. It's a world that then makes sense—challenging, life-altering sense, but sense nonetheless—of every other aspect of the world, from farming and fishing to politics and philosophy, from love and laughter to history and hope. Believing nonsense may be exciting for a moment, but it leaves you increasingly isolated.

Paul, and the people he knew whose lives had been transformed by the good news, found that what they believed—that the Messiah died for their sins in accordance with the Bible, that he was buried and raised—seemed to make them more alive, more aware of everything, more in tune with the whole of creation. Faith involves believing that certain things are true, of course. But (here's another caricature we have to put firmly to bed) this isn't about odd, detached dogmas. It's about certain things in the light of which everything else at last comes into focus. As C. S. Lewis once said—and this quote was chosen for his memorial tablet in Westminster Abbey—"I believe in Christianity as I believe that the sun has risen. Not only because I see it, but because by it I see everything else."

All this and more is what Paul meant when he spoke of the "power and wisdom" that became real through the announcement of the good news. To say it one more time, the message looks crazy and shameful when you try to fit it into any other way of looking at the world. But if you let it get inside you—or perhaps we should say, if *you* stand inside *it* and look out at the world—then suddenly you see everything else in a new way. A way that makes sense of everything—startling, shocking sense, a sudden and scary clarity. This is what Paul means by the "power" of this "good news." It does things to people. It transforms them.

What's more, they find—this is perhaps the oddest bit of all, but it was and is central—that this Jesus, this Messiah, *becomes personally present and real to them.* He's not just someone they are hearing *about.* It's as though he were standing beside them. This is the effect that the royal announcement, the good news, has on some, at least, of those who hear it. And with this sense of Jesus as present, alive, with them in a whole new way, all sorts of other things suddenly become clear. Those man-made idols with their temples scattered all around the city, places where all sorts of sordid things happen—suddenly these people know that's not the

[handwritten margin notes: How is God not a Jesus? Man-made idol? Jesus? + I can believe]

way to be human. They want to turn away entirely from that way of life. They want to find a new way to live.

When people find this happening to them, they are welcomed into a new family. (That's just as well, because in Paul's world, as in some parts of the world today, their own families may then reject them.) Within that family, they quickly learn how the gospel works out in practice. The announcement of what *has* happened—Jesus's death and resurrection as the fulfillment of the ancient biblical promises and divine purposes—is matched by the assurance of what *will* happen in the future, when God is "all in all," transforming the whole of creation and raising his people into new, transformed, bodily life. And held within those two poles, they learn that the life they now live in the present is to be transformed by its relation to the past and the future. Because Jesus died and was raised, those who belong to him have died and been raised, and they must live accordingly. Because God is going to remake the whole world and raise his people from the dead, they must live in the present in accordance with that ultimate promised destiny. Everything will be different.

In all of this, there is one thing we haven't yet mentioned directly, and it, too, is vital.

The Return of the One God

I have pointed out that in Paul's Roman world the word *gospel* was regularly used to speak about the royal announcement that was made when an emperor came to the throne, or perhaps on his birthday. That was the meaning everybody knew. Since Paul used words like *Lord* and phrases like *Son of God* to talk about Jesus—words and phrases that everybody knew belonged to the Roman emperors, not least because they were on coins and inscriptions—it would be easy to imagine that Paul spoke like that simply to indicate that Jesus was like Caesar only more so. But there is something deeper, older, and richer going on here.

In the Bible—the Bible in accordance with which the good news meant what it meant—the idea of good news is found in the book of Isaiah, chapters 40 and 52. And in Isaiah the good news is not simply about a coming Messiah. The good news is about *Israel's God himself,* the God they knew as YHWH, the God of Abraham, Isaac, and Jacob, the creator of the world.

So what is the good news about this God? How can there be news about *God*? Surely, if he's God, he's always simply God (so to speak). News implies that something new is happening; how can anything new happen to God?

The Bible sees all that quite differently. The God in whom the ancient Israelites believed was living and active, and that meant danger and drama as well as blessing. This God, who is really not at all like the God of today's popular imagination, had committed himself to working with and living among the Israelites—as long as they kept their side of the deal. But they didn't, and disaster struck. They were sent into exile, far from their own land. God himself (so they believed) abandoned the Temple in Jerusalem, leaving the place to its fate. Things couldn't get much worse. That was the backstory to the good news in Isaiah.

Isaiah's good news went like this: The one true God is on the move again! He has overcome all the powers of the world—the dark powers that enslave and corrupt and destroy genuine human life. He has overcome every obstacle that stands in the way of his people being restored to their land and their status as his people. And that means nothing can now stand in the way of his long-planned new creation. Finally all the ancient promises are going to come true. And in the middle of it all, at the heart of the good news, stands this promise: *this God is coming back in person, and all nations will see his glory.* This good news isn't about a mere human emperor. It is about the return of the true king, the God of all creation.

So what are we saying? Paul has taken biblical language about God and has applied it to the message about Jesus, knowing that in his hearers' minds it will resonate with language they associate with Caesar. If we can get our minds around that idea, we will be well on our way to understanding what he meant by the gospel.

Let's take it step by step. Paul believed that the return of YHWH had happened in Jesus. He believed that this continued to happen when he made the announcement about Jesus. God *had* come back in the person of Jesus; God *was* coming, to the whole world, in the presence and power of his Spirit whenever the good news was announced. And one day, God—the God now made known in Jesus—would come back to finish the task, to be all in all, to fill the world with his glory and love, to transform everything, to rectify everything, to heal everything with his powerful love.

That was the good news, according to the Bible and according to Paul. Something *had* happened. Something *would* happen. And in between, something powerful and mysterious *was happening* in the lives of all those who found themselves caught up in it. If we want to recapture the dynamic of the original early Christian gospel, we need to recapture this triple vision, and to see in particular what this tells us about the meaning of the word *God.* That is what this book is about. And it is also about the ways in which, in our day just as in Paul's, some find this good news a scandal and others find it boring nonsense, while still others discover that it unleashes God's power and unveils his wisdom.

3

———

Surprised by King Jesus

I T'S TIME NOW to hone in on the central figure of the story. Jesus himself remains one of the most compelling figures in all human history. No matter what your worldview, your beliefs, or your culture, you will find Jesus haunting, disturbing, and attractive.

That, however, merely puts him near the top of the list of compelling figures. We could all name others: Moses, the Buddha, Socrates, Muhammad. In more recent times, Mahatma Gandhi or Nelson Mandela. The ancient and modern worlds supply us with a range of choices. Most of these figures are evaluated in terms of the quality of advice they gave. Should we listen to this advice or not? Are they trusted guides for how we should live?

But the idea of good news poses a different sort of challenge. Jesus wasn't just a great character, a hero figure for subsequent generations to look up to. He was announcing good news— something that was happening and has now happened, something that changes the world. And either he was right or he was wrong. So what was this news, and in what sense was it good?

Jesus was not offering a teaching that could be compared with that of other teachers—though his teaching, as it stands, is truly remarkable. He was not offering a moral example, though if we want such a thing he remains outstanding. He was claiming to do things *through which the world would be healed, transformed, rescued, and renewed.* He was, in short, announcing good news, for Israel and the whole world.

His world, at least, was waiting for good news. The Jewish world of Jesus's day buzzed with speculation. Their great traditions told the story of the childless nomad Abraham, called by God to start a family through which the world would be rescued. This people would learn firsthand what rescue meant, since they would be enslaved in Egypt before being delivered by God in the Passover. God himself would lead them through the Red Sea, through years of wandering in the desert, until they finally inherited their promised land. That event (the exodus) remained central to Jewish life and thought. It shaped, and continues to shape, how Jews saw and see the world. It speaks of the one true God making himself known in power, defeating the powers of evil, and rescuing his people. It speaks of what, in later scriptures, came to be called the kingdom of God. In other words, it speaks of God *becoming* king of the world in a whole new way. The one true God was always the rightful ruler of the world, but he needed to reclaim his kingdom after the power of evil had usurped it.

Many people in Jesus's day believed that the time had come for this dream to turn into reality. This was the backstory for the good news they were eager to hear.

The exodus shaped Jesus, too. He shared the belief of his contemporaries (that the one God would finally rescue his people and the world through a new exodus) but with one big difference. He believed it was his own job to make it happen. This was his vocation, his special calling. People used to be bothered by the fact that Jesus talked about God but his followers talked later about

[handwritten marginal notes, left margin top:] others in modern day

[handwritten marginal notes, left margin bottom:] But Gods aren't always thought of as accepting all people

Jesus himself—as though the early Christians were doing something Jesus never intended. That is nonsense. Yes, Jesus talked about God. Of course. But he did so precisely *to explain what he himself was up to.* "If I'm casting out demons because I'm in league with God's spirit," he said when challenged, "well, then, God's kingdom has arrived on your doorstep!" (Matt. 12:28). He was claiming, in effect, to *be* the good news in person.

[handwritten: ✱ Then who created the universe?]

A Different Kind of King

That is why, throughout Jesus's public career, he talked about the good news of God's kingdom, redefining the idea of God's kingdom as he went along. God was coming back to take charge, he *[handwritten: ?]* said. *But it didn't look like what people had imagined.*

The idea of God becoming king was well known in Jesus's day. There should be no doubt about what it meant, because a number of ancient scriptural texts pointed in this direction. Many popular movements of Jesus's own day used the slogan, though Jesus gave it a different spin. Those popular movements, picking up the same scriptural promises that Jesus used, hoped for the moment we spoke of before: the moment of restoration, of Israel being rescued from enemies, of the new exodus.

The original exodus, many centuries before, had been what we would call a political revolution. In the old stories, it had involved Moses leading tens of thousands of slaves to escape into freedom. People in Jesus's day were looking for something equally important in terms of actual people, actual communities, actual newfound freedom. Some people proposed new leaders. Others thought that God himself would perform a mighty act of deliverance without human intervention. Some put the two together: human leaders had to get the people ready, then God would act. Or perhaps, others thought, God's people themselves had to act dramatically, in violent revolution against the wicked pagans. Perhaps that was how God wanted to accomplish his rescuing project. All this goes to show that *plenty of people wanted God to sort everything out and rescue his people, but nobody quite knew how it would happen.* They didn't ~~even~~ need to know.

Jesus thought he knew. He had what we would call a strong, clear sense of vocation. He believed that all this was happening, and would continue to happen, through his own work. That is why, in his day and even to this day, some people have thought he really was planning a violent revolution. Other kingdom movements were like that; surely Jesus slotted into that picture? But this is to misunderstand Jesus. Part of the strangeness of the good news—part of the reason people don't understand it to this day—is that Jesus refused to fit the pattern. Not because he was awkward or obstinate, or wanted to do things differently for the sake of it. Rather, he had a different vision of God, God's purposes, and God's way of achieving those purposes—a different vision of what the real good news was supposed to be.

Here Jesus was walking a tightrope. People longed to hear about a kingdom of God that would come through military and social revolution. They'd had that kind of thing before, two hundred years earlier. They would have it again: the first in the sixties of the first century and the last in the 130s, with smaller outbreaks of revolt in between. Such things were in the air. People wanted them. If Jesus had given the word, plenty of folk would have hammered their farming tools into swords and signed up.

Everything we know about Jesus makes it clear not only that he didn't go that route but that he warned against it. He saw such nationalist revolutions as part of the problem. He regarded them as telltale signs that his fellow Jews had radically misunderstood what their God was all about, what their God was *like*. Their

NoT everythings

How can we have more than 1 overall life force?

would-be rebellion against Rome was a symptom of their rebellion against God, against their vocation to be the light of the nations. Part of the point of Jesus's famous Sermon on the Mount was to recall Israel to that vocation.

Equally, some people in Jesus's day reacted the other way. They wanted to step back altogether from the public arena. Hide in the desert, say your prayers, and God will do whatever God wants to do. Or study the scriptures and try to keep them as best you can, but do so as a matter of private piety, not public policy. These alternatives are also well known in our day. Jesus set his face against both of them. They constitute advice, not news. He had come to say that God was on the move, that God was becoming king, that God was accomplishing the new exodus, that this was the long-awaited good news that would change everything. You can't stay quiet about good news. *what is a King? person?*

Jesus didn't stay quiet. He was constantly telling stories (parables) to explain, as only subtle and challenging short stories can, that the way God was becoming king was very different. And equally important, he was constantly *doing* things that showed what God's new world was going to look like. People were healed—a sign of new creation reaching out to embrace actual human bodies and lives. People found forgiveness, as the power of new creation reached into their moral and spiritual lives with the warm assurance of God's love. People who had seen themselves at the bottom of the pile, economically, socially, morally, and physically, suddenly found their lives turned upside down. Wherever Jesus went, there was a party. It's obvious why.

It's also obvious that many would object. All this was upsetting the expected order. When Jesus overturned the moneychangers' tables in the temple, he accomplished in one gesture what he'd been doing to people's cherished assumptions for the previous two or three years. His vision of what it would look like when God became king was quite different from the way most other people saw it—including, it seems, his own family, who on at least one occasion decided he was out of his mind. Even his closest friends didn't understand what he was up to.

Nor would they, until the end. What Jesus was doing only made sense in light of his belief about where it would all end. He had a clear sense of vocation about that, too—about what he must do to bring matters to a head. He chose the exodus moment, the Passover feast, to do what had to be done. This, he believed, was how the good news would become a reality. Jewish life revolved around and was shaped by the first exodus. What Jesus did and said made it clear that he intended to accomplish a second exodus, which would play the same role but for the whole world.

Let's put it like this.

The Jewish people of the first century were expecting their God to come back in person to rescue them, revealing his glorious presence, defeating their enemies, and reestablishing them as his people once and for all.

They got Jesus.

They were hoping for a new exodus—that is, a repeat performance of what had happened fifteen hundred years earlier, when the Israelites had been enslaved in Egypt and their God (they believed) came to rescue them. He had overcome the powerful Egyptian rulers, liberated his people, and led them in person through the Sinai Desert to bring them to the promised land. Many prophets had said that one day God would do something like this again. Many people were hoping it would be soon.

They got Jesus.

They were hoping for a new age of justice and peace. Ancient scriptures had spoken of a time when the wolf would lie down with the lamb, the mountains would drip sweet wine, and the earth would be full of the knowledge and the glory of the one true God like waters filling the sea.

They got Jesus.

Is it any wonder they were puzzled?

In one story, on the third day after his death, two of his close friends explain sadly to a stranger that they had hoped was the one who would redeem Israel. The point was, they crucified him, so he can't have been the one to do it after all. We must have been mistaken.

Jesus's cousin John also believed he had a vocation. His job was to get people ready for the great coming act of divine deliverance. He, too, seems to have been echoing the original exodus, when God brought his people through the Red Sea, then across the river Jordan, into their promised land. So John was plunging people into the river Jordan to get people ready for this new exodus. To start the process, perhaps. The Greek word for "plunging" is *baptizo*, from which we get *baptize*. Hence John's nickname: John the Baptizer or John the Baptist.

But John, too, quickly became puzzled. He wondered if he'd been mistaken. Was this really the good news for which he'd been waiting?

John himself had been announcing good news, or at least that good news was on the way. God was about to do what he'd promised. Since that great day was about to dawn, everybody should get ready, in case the sun should rise and find them still asleep. But once Jesus's public career got underway and John heard what his cousin was doing, he seems to have been horribly disappointed. By then, John had been put in prison for denouncing Herod, the local ruler. He had hoped, of course, that Jesus's message about God's new day would mean that he would be set free to share in the festivities. So he sent Jesus a message: Are you really the one? Did I miss the point? Is there perhaps someone else coming after you who will *really* do the business?

Jesus's own cousin didn't realize what was going on; nor did the other John, who, with his brother James, was one of Jesus's closest associates. The two of them approached, bold as brass, requesting from Jesus the right to sit in places of honor and power at his right and his left when he came into his kingdom. That shows the kind of thing people around Jesus were expecting.

Jesus gave a gentle and cryptic answer to John the Baptist: look what's happening and draw your own conclusions. He gave a crisp answer to James and John: The rulers of the world run things one way, but we're going to run things another way. Ordinary rulers do it through ordinary power. They give themselves airs and get their way by threats and bullying. We're going to do it, he said, by loving and serving. This is how it had to be, he went on, because (referring to himself and his Bible-based vocation), "The son of man didn't come to be waited on. He came to be the servant, to give his life 'as a ransom for many'" (Mark 10:45).

Jesus was quoting from Isaiah, from the heart of the good news passage. This was how the great plan was to be accomplished. The good news Jesus announced was that the plan was now being put into effect. The good news the early church announced *about* Jesus was the message that the plan *had been* put into effect. It had worked.

This is central to the good news Jesus announced. It isn't just that God is becoming king, through Jesus and what he is doing, but that *God's kingship is a different sort of kingship altogether.* There is a different kind of power, and it is the power of the gospel— the power announced by the gospel, the power wielded by the gospel. It is the power neither of brute force nor of superior argument but of something that goes much deeper, into every area of human life. The early Christians called it the power of *agape*. Our modern word *love* doesn't begin to get near what they meant by that, but it will have to do for the moment as a signpost to a great, multidimensional, all-embracing energy, which swept people off their feet in the first century and continues to do so today.

The Power of Love

The clash between Jesus and the powers of the world—between the kingdom of God and the kingdom of humans—was never about God simply having a bit more power than humans, so that he could manage to beat them at their own game. It isn't that God has stronger tanks and bombs than everybody else. That's what people expected in Jesus's day (well, they didn't have tanks and bombs, but you know what I mean). It is also what people expect, and often want, today. ("Why doesn't God do something to stop wicked dictators killing people?") This is why the good news is so often misunderstood. This is why it continues to puzzle and challenge people, as it always did. It's also why people step back from the big claims in the Bible and turn the radical good news into something they find more believable. Something about "me and my relationship to God" or about "going to heaven." Something more like advice than news.

Let's be clear. The relationship each of us has with God is hugely important. It is also vital to insist that God will indeed look after his people following their deaths, all the way to his final new creation. But these are not the center of the good news. We have placed the stress at the wrong point, like people putting the em*pha*sis on the wrong syl*lab*le. The words may be true, but the way we say them gets in the way of that truth coming out clearly. The good news is about the living God overcoming all the powers of the world to establish his rule of justice and peace, *on earth as in heaven*. Not in heaven, later on. And that victory is won not by superior power of the same kind but by a different sort of power altogether.

We know what the power of the world looks like. When push comes to shove, as it often does, it is the power of violence, using the threat of pain and death. It is, yes, the power of tanks and bombs, and also of guns and knives and whips and prisons and barbed wire and bulldozers. Weapons to destroy people's lives; machines to destroy their homes. Cruelty in the home or at work. Malice and manipulation where there should be gentleness, kindness, and wisdom. Jesus's power is of a totally different sort, as he explained to the Roman governor a few minutes before the governor sent him to his death—thereby proving the point. The kingdoms of the world run on violence. The kingdom of God, Jesus declared, runs on love.

That is the good news.

This wasn't a theory. It was and is a general truth, but the only reason for believing it is that it actually happened. In history. "The son of God," wrote Paul in one of his earliest letters, "loved me and gave himself for me" (Gal. 2:20). There are a thousand ways of explaining what exactly that meant; that's for another time. For now we need to know simply this. Jesus of Nazareth went to his death believing that this would be the ultimate good-news moment. This was when the Creator's plan to rescue Israel, humans, and the whole world would come at last to its strange, dark conclusion. That was the climax of the good news Jesus came to announce and embody. Jesus on the cross was the ultimate good news in person.

We could go on. Albert Schweitzer, a century or more ago, used another strong image. Jesus, he said, was like a man convinced the wheel of history was going to turn in the opposite direction. He waited for this to happen, but it didn't. Then he threw himself upon the wheel, and it crushed him—but it did indeed start to turn in the other direction.

All these images speak of *the strange victory of the new king* over the powers of evil. This is the moment of the messianic victory. As the four Gospels indicate, it comes down in the last analysis to a battle between Jesus, as the pioneer of God's kingdom on earth as in heaven, and the accuser, the satan, the dark quasi-personal force bent on destroying God's work, God's kingdom, God's world. And now God's son. The satan does its worst, piling up false accusations, betrayals, and unjust judgments against Jesus. Evil, in this quasi-personal sense, grows at last to its full height. It reveals its true self, in all its horror. *And at that moment, the divine sentence of condemnation is pronounced upon it.* Upon evil itself.

It isn't just that Jesus somehow survives, lives (as it were) to fight another day. The resurrection doesn't simply mean, "Well, he took it all and somehow came through unscathed." Jesus was *not* unscathed. He didn't "survive." He really suffered. He really bled and died. The resurrection doesn't mean that the death didn't matter or wasn't real. What the resurrection reveals—apart from new creation, obviously, to which we will return—is that *on the cross evil itself was condemned.* The power of evil had taken Jesus over, had worked into every fiber of his being through the moral and spiritual violence done to him, as well as the physical torment. What looked like a judicial punishment meted out upon Jesus was in fact a judicial punishment—an actual sentence of death—meted out *upon evil itself.* Several writers in the New Testament make this point from various angles, but as usual, it is Paul who puts it most sharply. "God sent his own son," he writes, "in the likeness of sinful flesh, and as a sin-offering; and, right there in the flesh, *he condemned sin*" (Rom. 8:3, emphasis added). This is why he can say, "There is no condemnation for those in the Messiah, Jesus!" (Rom. 8:1). Sin has been condemned; punishment has been meted out. Therefore sinners who are now "in the Messiah" can be confident that there is "no condemnation" for them. We note, by the way, that though Paul very clearly sees Jesus's death here as both *penal* (this was a judicial sentence) and *substitutionary* (Jesus dies, therefore we do not die), he does *not* say

Not of course not!

that God punished Jesus. That would be an oversimplification, and it lends itself to distortion. Stick with the big picture. On the cross, God passed the sentence of death on evil itself.

This, then, was the victory of the king. This is why the kingdom of God, which Jesus had launched in his public career, was inaugurated in a whole new way with his death and resurrection. What was holding back the kingdom was the dark power, the force of evil itself? On the cross, that force, that power was defeated. All it can now do is shout and scream and flail about in its death throes. True, that can still be terrible and destructive. We all know this, in our own lives and in the wider world. But the early Christians—who themselves knew only too well that the world had not turned into Utopia overnight and that they still faced suffering, prison, and death—firmly believed that what had happened on the cross was *the Messianic victory.* That is why they told the story the way they did. When we say today that "the Messiah died for our sins," this is close to the heart of what we should mean.

What the Resurrection Reveals

If that had been the end, however, it wouldn't have been good news at all. It would only have meant one more failed messiah. The only reason the death of Jesus was ever thought of as good news was because of what happened next.

Without Easter—that is, without Jesus being raised from the dead into a new bodily life—nobody would ever have imagined that God's saving plan had been fulfilled. No first-century Jew would ever have said that the shameful execution of a would-be leader could complete the centuries-old, long-prophesied new exodus, rescuing Israel from its long exile and the human race from sin and death. The Jews of the day did, from time to time, tell stories about suffering, describing righteous martyrs whose tribulations would somehow contribute to God's eventual plan. But one more martyr wouldn't mean that the kingdom of God *had* come. It would mean that it hadn't. Israel, and the world, would still be waiting.

Without Easter, in fact, the movement that came into existence around Jesus would not have been about good *news*. At most, it would have been about good *advice* ("Here's how Jesus taught us to live our lives"). Some might well doubt whether this advice was actually good in the first place: look what happened to Jesus himself! But even if the advice was good, it would still mean that people were waiting for the great day to dawn, not that they were celebrating its arrival.

That is clearly what Jesus's first followers thought after his death. "We were hoping that he was going to redeem Israel," say the two on the road to Emmaus (Luke 24:21). But they knew that his crucifixion had ended those hopes.

So how can we come to terms with what the first Christians said happened next? We need to remember two things in particular.

First, the word *resurrection* always meant bodies. Numerous teachers in the ancient world developed ways of saying that even if someone's body was in a tomb, something else—perhaps a soul, though that's one of the most slippery words around—was still alive somewhere. But that was never what *resurrection* meant. That word was not a fancy way for talking about life after death. It always referred to a new bodily life *after* a period of being bodily dead. The ancient world, like the modern world, produced widely differing speculations about what happens after we die. The word *resurrection* designates one and only one of those options: a new bodily existence. A new physical human being, after a time during which that human being had been dead and gone. (Two or three hundred years after Jesus, some speculative writings picked up the word *resurrection* and used it for a non-bodily life after death. That was deliberately polemical. In the early decades, where the basic evidence is found, the meaning was constant.)

Second, Jews were the only people in the ancient world who believed that God would eventually raise the dead—that is, bring them back to some new sort of bodily life as part of his promise to renew the whole creation. (This, by the way, is not reincarnation. People often get confused on this point. Reincarnation is about a dead person coming back as somebody else. In resurrection, people retain their own identity and receive a radically renewed body as its appropriate physical expression.) Though this belief was unique to Jews, however, not all Jews shared it. The conservative elite who ran the Temple, always wary of dangerous innovations, rejected the idea of resurrection; if people believe that sort of thing, they thought, who knows what they'll come up with? But in the time of Jesus, bodily resurrection was the mainstream popular belief. It's reflected in the burial customs of the period, a telling sign.

But—and this is one of the most important points—this resurrection was to be something that would happen to *everybody,* at the very end of everything. Nobody envisaged that it might happen to one person in the middle of history. Yes, in the ancient scriptures there are stories of people being raised from the dead, but those were one-offs, as when Jesus raised Lazarus and one or two other people. Such people would have to die again, whereas the whole point of the resurrection was that it would be forever.

At this point people sometimes jump to the wrong conclusion. "Well," they say, "the Jews were expecting resurrection, so after Jesus died it was natural for them to imagine that this was what had happened." That simply doesn't work. The resurrection they expected was something God would do for all his people at the very end, not for one person in advance of the rest. In any case,

of what?

that suggestion would prove too much. Lots of other Jewish leaders were killed by the authorities within two hundred years on
either side of Jesus. People sometimes said of such unfortunate
heroes that they *would* be raised from the dead. They never said
that they *had* been already. Followers of an executed leader either
found another leader or gave up the movement. Jesus's followers
did neither. They declared that he was Israel's Messiah and the
world's rightful Lord. You can't explain that unless you say they
really did believe that the unimaginable had happened—that he
had been bodily raised from the dead.

For the Jews, as for the early Christians, belief in resurrection
drew together two other foundational beliefs. First, God was the
creator of all things who had made a world full of beauty and
power. Second, God intended to sort out the mess into which the
world had fallen. He would judge it—that is, he would get rid of
everything that corrupted and defaced it, in order to renew it and
make it, even more gloriously, what it was supposed to be. Creation and judgment thus meet in resurrection. That's when the
Creator says yes to his world and no to all that damages, distorts,
or destroys it.

now Climate change ?

So what made the early Christians say (as all of them did) that
Jesus had been raised from the dead? And why should anybody
then, or anybody now, take seriously such an extraordinary claim?

The answer the early Christians give comes in different forms,
but central to them all is the story, summarized in Paul's short-
hand gospel, about the Messiah dying, being buried, and then
being raised. That is, of course, a brief summary. In the four Gospels, we get longer versions. Interestingly, these show no signs of
being copied from one another. Elsewhere in the four Gospels, it
looks as though the writers knew one another's work or at least
shared common traditions. In the resurrection stories, they seem
quite independent—so much so that, like witnesses at a trial, they
often disagree about superficial details while retaining a strong

grip on the central point. Anyway, the story they tell involves two things that are closely intertwined. First, the tomb was empty. Second, Jesus appeared to his followers and talked and ate with them.

These two go together. By itself, an empty tomb in the ancient world would mean grave robbery. People often put valuable objects in tombs. Some had seen Jesus as a potentially royal figure, making his tomb a likely target. (The tomb in question, by the way, wasn't like a modern grave, a trench dug in the ground and then filled in. It was a cave with a ledge. The idea was that later, when the flesh had decomposed, the bones would be collected and stored elsewhere.) By itself, therefore, an empty tomb would simply mean that thieves had been at work. It would carry no hint of resurrection.

In the same way, an appearance of someone recently dead by itself would be understood in terms of ghosts or similar apparitions. There are many well-authenticated stories in the modern world, as well as in the ancient world, about recently dead persons appearing to friends or family members. I know of two such stories in the late twentieth century, one in my own family. And here's the point. First, the ancient world had an accepted language for such things. An apparition like that, they would think, might be a ghost, a phantasm, or even an angel. They never used the word *resurrection* for such a phenomenon. This is because, second, such an event doesn't show that the person concerned has come back to life. Precisely the opposite. It shows that the person in question really is dead. There is a story in the book of Acts about Peter escaping certain death and turning up at the house where the church was praying for his release. Hearing his voice, they say, "It must be his angel!"—in other words, he must have been killed, and this is a ghostly visitation, as it were, coming to say goodbye. This did not mean he had been raised from the dead. It was clear confirmation that he hadn't been.

So an empty tomb by itself and appearances by themselves would only help establish that the dead person really was dead. But put the two together and the result is explosive. Jesus's first followers were just as astonished as we would be. They knew the laws of nature as well as we do. Every ancient non-Jewish writer who mentions the possibility of resurrection dismisses it as impossible. The best explanation for the evidence we have is that Jesus of Nazareth, on the third day after he was brutally executed by those professional killers, the Roman soldiers, was found to be very thoroughly and bodily alive again, though with a new sort of body that seemed to have new properties.

This is perhaps the strangest thing about the stories. Many people have suggested that these descriptions of the risen Jesus were cobbled together later in the century as pious fictions to sustain the early Christian movement. Had that been the case, the Jesus of such stories would surely have been recognized at once. His followers had spent a long time in his close company, day and night. And yet, in the stories we have, they don't always recognize the risen Jesus. He is the same, yet somehow different. This is unprecedented. You wouldn't make up tales like these. No ancient biblical prophecies mention such a possibility.

What's more, the very stories in which the risen Jesus eats food and invites people to touch him are the stories in which he appears and disappears through locked doors and finally ascends into heaven. The very stories (in other words) that seem to be trying to say, "Look, he really was physically present," also tell us things that make us say, "But ordinary bodies don't do that." If these are stories invented to convince people that Jesus had come back into exactly the same life as before, they don't do a very good job.

But there are many signs that the stories were not, after all, invented out of thin air. One such sign is the place of the women in all four Gospels. Mary Magdalene and other women were first at the empty tomb, first to meet the risen Jesus, first to tell others they'd seen him. Nobody in the ancient world, wanting to convince skeptics, would have made that up. Women were not regarded as credible witnesses. Already by the time of Paul's first letter to Corinth (the early fifties AD), the official tradition had airbrushed the women out of the record. For official purposes, they were an embarrassment. Yet there they are in Matthew, Mark, Luke, and—especially—John.

I have said before that without the resurrection of Jesus there is no good news. Without the resurrection, there is nothing to say that the crucifixion itself accomplished any of the things we discussed in the preceding chapters. Thousands of young Jews were crucified by the Romans over the course of the first century. Why should this death have meant anything more than theirs did? Their deaths meant, not that the kingdom of God had come, but precisely that it hadn't. That was why the two disciples on the road to Emmaus were so depressed. They had hoped that he was the one to redeem Israel, but the crucifixion had appeared to put an end to all that.

But the resurrection of Jesus—without which it is straightforwardly impossible to explain the rise of early Christianity at all—must then be seen in a particular light. Here again, as with the cross, it is possible to set it, as a fragment, within the wrong narrative. It is possible to reconstruct the scene so that the resurrection, though firmly believed, means something quite different from what it means in the New Testament. We need a different framework for the whole story.

The Real Good News

First, though, the inadequate and misleading accounts. Jesus's resurrection does not mean that God somehow gave him a free pass on a personal basis, either because he was God's son or for any other reason. The resurrection was not a special favor granted to Jesus and somehow, meanly, withheld from everybody else. It was not a special miracle, a supernatural sign to demonstrate that Jesus was divine. To tell the story like that, as many have done, would imply that God is capable of stepping in to do one-off bizarre tricks when he feels like it, which quite reasonably makes people wonder why he hasn't stepped in to prevent some of the truly awful things that have happened in human history, not least of which were in the last century. The question of God's moral governance of the world is a large and difficult issue, but to call it into question on the basis of a misleading way of telling the story of Easter is unnecessary and unhelpful.

Nor is it the case that the resurrection of Jesus somehow proves something called life after death. Most first-century Jews believed, in any case, that God would look after them following their death. They spoke frequently about their belief that those who had died, especially those who had died as martyrs, *would* be raised from the dead in the future. Nobody thought one person would be raised ahead of everyone else within the ongoing world.

In any case, resurrection was not precisely life after death. It's hard to know what to say about where Jesus was between the afternoon of Good Friday and the morning of Easter Day. His body was in the tomb, but he had said to the brigand crucified beside him, "You'll be with me in paradise, this very day" (Luke 23:43). Nobody explains what *paradise* means. It's the only time that word is used in the New Testament. Whatever it was, *that* was life after death; resurrection was a further step, a huge leap forward into a kind of existence never before known. It was life *after* life after death, a new bodily life *following* the brief period of life after death, whether in paradise or elsewhere.

The resurrection of Jesus, then, is not first and foremost about going to heaven. Neither Matthew, Mark, Luke, nor John even mention heaven in their accounts of Jesus's resurrection. The ascension, described by Luke, means something quite different from what people mean when they say that someone who has died has gone to heaven. The ascension means that, as Matthew says, all authority in heaven and on earth has now been given to Jesus. The heaven to which he ascends—heaven basically means "God's space," which in biblical cosmology intersects with earth, our space—is the control room, the place from which everything is now run.

The resurrection of Jesus does not, then, simply give comfort to those who face death, whether their own or that of someone they love. It does that, and various writers in the New Testament apply it that way. But that is not its primary meaning. Once again, if you take an element of the good news and put it into a different story, you make it mean something it didn't quite mean, and you miss the meaning it was supposed to have in the first place. The main point of the resurrection is that it is the beginning of God's new world.

The point, in any case, is not to force someone to believe, to fit in this odd new possibility ("Jesus was raised from the dead?!") on the outer edge of their worldview, along with, say, the possibility of life on Mars or a perpetual-motion machine. The point is that today, as in Paul's day, when people announce that Jesus of Nazareth was crucified and raised from the dead, that he was and is Israel's Messiah and the world's rightful Lord, then things happen. Back to C. S. Lewis again: people come to believe this, not necessarily because we can fully understand it (we can't) but because once you get that straight you can understand all sorts of other things. Believe in Jesus's resurrection, and we can make sense of God, of the world, of ourselves. Or rather, with this in place we discover that God has (so to speak) made sense of us. Sorted us out. Cleaned us up, dusted us down, turned us inside out. Made genuine humans of us. That's what the message of the crucified and risen Jesus has always done. That's what it still does.

According to whom?

So how might we in turn summarize the good news—both the good news announced by Jesus and the good news that his first followers announced when they talked about him later on? The good news is that *the one true God has now taken charge of the world, in and through Jesus and his death and resurrection.* The ancient hopes have indeed been fulfilled, but in a way nobody imagined. God's plan to put the world right has finally been launched. He has grasped the world in a new way, to sort it out and fill it with his glory and justice, as he always promised. But he has done so in a way beyond the wildest dreams of prophecy. The ancient sickness that had crippled the whole world, and humans with it, has been cured at last, so that new life can rise up in its place. Life has come to life and is pouring out like a mighty river into the world, in the form of a new power, the power of love. The good news was, and is, that all this *has* happened in and through Jesus; that one day it *will* happen, completely and utterly, to all creation; *and that we humans, every single one of us, whoever we are, can be caught up in that transformation here and now.* This is the Christian gospel. Do not allow yourself to be fobbed off with anything less.

4

Distorted and
Competing Gospels

BUT IS IT *true*? Many readers who have followed the argument to this point find this question bubbling up from the depths of their minds and hearts. So many things in our culture, our media, our world as a whole put enormous pressure on us to say, well, perhaps Jesus really was a remarkable man, but we can't be sure if he did or said half the things the old texts say, and we certainly can't know that the whole package happened like that. Surely the best we can do is to see Jesus as a distant if impressive teacher and leader. Do we have to speak of an *event* that has actually changed the world? And isn't that in any case a ridiculous idea?

In this chapter I want to try to answer these and similar objections. In particular, I want to suggest that part of the problem lies in the way well-meaning Christian teachers, over many generations, have put the emphasis in the wrong place. Subtle distortions have crept in. What people say they can't believe is quite often not exactly what classic Christianity ought to be affirming. Sorting this out takes patience, and I hope this chapter will reward it. Yes, this good news goes on being a scandal to some and foolish nonsense to others, as Paul said, but at least we can understand why that should be so.

Can We Trust the Gospels?

Let's start with the obvious problem. Can we trust the Gospels? Answering that properly would take another whole book, and indeed I've written one or two on that topic. Despite a continuing chorus of skepticism, I and many other scholars who have studied the material intensively within its first-century context have come to the conclusion that these stories are basically trustworthy.

That isn't to say that we can "prove" everything in them. Of course we can't. Hardly anything in history works like that. The demand for proof often comes from people who have scientific proof in mind. But that's not how history works. Science normally studies things we can repeat: experiments, observations, laboratory tests. History necessarily studies things that cannot be repeated. It works from evidence and looks for high probability about what caused that evidence. Like science, however, history works by hypothesis and verification. That is to say, you look at the evidence, come up with a larger picture within which the event might make sense, and then test that larger picture once more against the evidence and modify it as necessary—or perhaps abandon it and start again.

Science does this all the time. People who work at the cutting edge in, say, physics are constantly adjusting their big picture, sometimes modifying it quite radically, but that doesn't mean suddenly water is going to boil at 90 degrees Celsius instead of

100. In the same way, historians of the first century are forever studying texts, old coins, archaeological evidence, and so on, and coming up with new theories about what happened and why, but that doesn't mean one day we will decide Jerusalem was not after all destroyed by the Romans in AD 70—or that Jesus of Nazareth was not after all crucified roughly forty years before that.

In fact, like most things in life that really matter—love, beauty, justice—you can't *prove* things in history the way you can prove Pythagoras's theorem. But there are lots of things you can be certain of nonetheless.

what is this?

Jesus's life, his announcement of God's kingdom, his radical redefinition of that kingdom, and his death on a Roman cross—we can be certain of all that. Few serious historians of any background or belief would deny those facts.

Jesus's resurrection falls into a different category. Not because it wasn't a historical event in the sense of something that actually happened in history. But because if it *did* happen, it set a new standard for our understanding of the way the world is. Lots of events do that in smaller ways. Splitting the atom. Space travel. The discovery of America. Everything looks different once those have happened. After them, you can't fit new discoveries into your previous picture of the way the world is. Jesus's resurrection is like that, only much, much more so.

But the rest of Jesus's life—his teachings, his healings, and so on—can be broadly accepted as historical. They weren't made up decades later as clever or pious fiction. Skeptical scholars have tried to make that case for generations and have again and again been answered by patient and serious historical work. There isn't the time or space here to rehearse all the arguments. Those who want to follow up will find plenty of material for doing so.

Let us, however, just note one point. This is important in itself, and it also looks ahead to the problem we always face when we try to make things clear.

The stories about Jesus constantly portray him as saying things that even his family and friends didn't understand. There is a high probability that this is historically accurate. Jesus's early followers were under pressure to tell his story as clearly as possible. If, despite that, they went on telling stories about how his hearers didn't understand what he was doing, or how people had hoped for one thing only to be confronted with something different, this must be because that kind of puzzled reaction had been deeply embedded in the memories everybody had of Jesus's public career. By the time the stories were written down, Jesus's followers had sorted it all out more clearly in their minds. But they still told the stories of how, during his lifetime, people were going around saying things like, "But we had hoped . . ." In other words, *when Jesus himself was telling the good news as he saw it, there were plenty of people who found it so different from what they expected that they just couldn't see it.* That is a strange historical fact, but a fact it certainly is. And it demands that we understand all sorts of other things in its light.

Curiously, on the day I edited this chapter into its final form, I received an e-mail from a stranger raising exactly this question. It all seems so complicated, he said. Why couldn't God—or Jesus!—have put it more simply? The best answer must be that Jesus believed his contemporaries—even his Jewish contemporaries, and how much more his non-Jewish ones!—had their heads and hearts full of wrong ideas, and he constantly ran the risk that they would hear what he was saying within the context of those wrong ideas and so twist it completely out of shape. Actually, this goes on being a problem all through history. Jesus's message *to* his contemporaries, and the church's message *about* Jesus, never fit what people expect. Often enough, they don't fit what the church itself expects. I will return to that in a moment. *The good news is always different from what people think it will be.* Sometimes it's so different that they can't begin to recognize it. That is why, as Paul said, it is foolish to some and scandalous to others. Sometimes it's so different that they are afraid of it, or hate it, or try to stamp it out.

Some early Christian thinkers, recognizing this problem, developed an understanding of why such a phenomenon might occur. How we understand things is a function of our whole personality. But if that whole personality is significantly flawed in some way—and sadly, that seems to be the case with all of us—this will affect the mental framework with which we start. It isn't, in other words, that we are flawed human beings in other respects but our minds are clear and fully operational, just waiting like a blank sheet of paper for someone to write true ideas on them. Our minds, which are intimately connected with our imaginations, our emotions, and our physical bodies in a rich and multitextured combination, need to be sorted out just like the rest of us. If we insist on keeping our mental, emotional, and imaginative world the way it's always been, the good news just won't fit. We will then either reject it or distort it, cutting off the bits we can't fit in or reshaping parts to conform to the ideas we already have. In this chapter and later on, I will explain some ways that has happened in recent centuries.

Of course, this could just be a cop-out: "You don't understand my message because your hearts and minds are so messed up." Anyone could say that when in fact they were talking nonsense. The question then is, if people allow the good news to remake and reshape their mental, imaginary, and emotional worlds, will they end up in a bigger muddle than before? Or will they become fuller, more whole human beings? Jesus is quoted as saying that he came so people could have life, "full to overflowing" (John 10:10). If the good news has that effect, especially on people whose previous life was indeed seriously messed up, then the original claim looks that much stronger.

Here, then, is a paradox, but an important one. One of the things we certainly know about Jesus is that people found him both compelling and puzzling. He was not, in other words, the sort of teacher who was simply adding to people's store of knowledge. Nor was he explaining a new formula for how to go to heaven to people who might have had wrong ideas on the subject. He wasn't giving new or more detailed answers to questions they were already asking. He was doing and saying things designed to tease his hearers into facing new and dangerous questions, into looking at familiar ideas (such as the kingdom of God) from new and unexpected angles. Most people, then and now, find that disturbing and try to avoid it.

That is as far as we can go for the moment with this opening question about the reliability of the early stories regarding Jesus. But when we think of the kingdom of God, one of the central things Jesus was talking about, we face another familiar question. How can we use the word *kingdom* today?

A Different Kind of Kingdom

Americans often tell me this. "We used to have kings," they say, "but we gave them up. You British understand these things; we don't." This is a misunderstanding. The constitutional monarchy we have today in the United Kingdom is quite different from ancient monarchies. In fact, the president of the United States is, in some ways, more like an ancient king than any British head of state has been for a long time. But that's not the point. When we use the word *king,* we are not buying in to one particular kind of kingship, whether ancient or modern. Here, as elsewhere, Jesus deliberately forced people to look from fresh and disturbing angles at things they thought they knew about already.

The models of kingship in Jesus's day were not exactly encouraging. Neither Caesar in Rome nor Herod in Galilee was a good example of what Jesus meant when he spoke of kingship or kingdom, of God's kingship or God's kingdom. Indeed, more than once he contrasted God's kingship with the ordinary human sort. We saw earlier how he made the point sharply to James and John: Human rulers do things one way, but we're going to do them a different way. For us, power comes through service, particularly through self-sacrifice. *The reason Jesus went on talking about* kingdom, *despite the obvious risks of misunderstanding in his own day, was because he wanted to replace the ordinary sort of kingdom with a quite different sort.*

Jesus wasn't content to leave existing structures in place and start up a nice, quiet, unobtrusive movement somewhere else. He didn't want the rest of the world to go on with its idea of kingship while he started a sect, a separatist movement that wouldn't challenge that notion. That might have been the effect of allowing human rulers to keep the word *king* while choosing a different slogan altogether. What he was doing was far more radical. Not only was Jesus plugging in to the ancient scriptural promises that spoke of God coming back at last to be king of his people and the whole world. He was insisting that this kingdom of God, this new reality, the heart of his good news, was a different sort of rule based on a different sort of power. *And that it was designed to challenge the present powers of the world with a new kingship that would trump theirs altogether.*

I sometimes wonder whether people who object to Jesus's language about kingship are really hankering after a world in which nobody will be in charge of anything. Like the Dwarfs in C. S. Lewis's *The Last Battle*, they don't want Tash, the foreign god, to be their ruler, but neither do they want Aslan, their rightful lord. "The Dwarfs are for the Dwarfs." For such people, the idea of God being king basically means God being a tyrant. *But the whole point of Jesus's good news is that the one true God is not a tyrant.* Tyranny is not the only form of kingship. Look back at the ancient scriptures, particularly the great song about kingship we know as Psalm 72. There the whole point of being a king—the way a true king is counted as legitimate—is that he listens to the plight of the poor and does something about it.

Part of the good news is that the God who has taken charge of the world is the God of utter, self-giving, lavish, and generous love. It is we who have twisted the notion of power so that now the only thing it means for us is bullying and tyranny. But to look at the true God that way—as, tragically, many have done, both inside the church and outside—is to trim the true God down to the model of fake little pagan gods, out for their own ends, trying to throw their weight about, ready to make life unpleasant for any who get in the way. The true picture of God is right at the center of the good news.

These questions—about the reliability of the Gospels and the ideas of king and kingdom—are important. But they only scratch the surface. There are three other, much larger, problems that prevent those in our time from grasping the idea of good news that I set out in the previous chapter.

The first has to do with the way the church has presented all this for the last thousand years or so. The second has to do with the way modern Western culture has conditioned the church to think in certain ways that have people looking in the wrong direction. The third has to do with the way Western culture has, for at least two centuries, drip-fed us a belief that, as long as we hold it (and especially if we hold it without realizing that it *is* a belief at all!), makes it straightforwardly impossible for us to believe that the events concerning Jesus really were the good news around which the whole world, and its whole history, actually revolve.

Turning the Good News into Bad News

The first of these, then, has to do with the popular view of what Christianity is all about—and when I say the popular view, I mean the view of most people inside the church as well as outside. Most people in the Western world think of Christianity as a system: a religious system, a system of salvation, or a system of morality. Most people do not think of it as news—a message about something that happened, as a result of which everything is now different. Insofar as they use the word *gospel* at all—which, as we saw, is an old English word that means "good news"—they use it with meanings that have moved away from the idea of news as such. The four Gospels in the Bible, Matthew, Mark, Luke, and John, were originally written precisely to say, "This is what just happened, and everything is forever different as a result." But when people speak of the Gospels today, they usually just mean the four books about Jesus. When people talk about preaching the gospel, they regularly mean explaining to people how they can become Christians, or perhaps explaining what it means that Christ died for their sins, or indeed telling people how to be sure of going to heaven. All of that, of course, is important. But it is not the good news, the thing itself.

In particular, the church has latched onto a way of speaking about the gospel that goes like this: you are a sinner, deserving death; Jesus died in your place; therefore believe in him, and you'll go to heaven after all. This can be shortened even further to something like, Jesus took my punishment. This assumes, first, that I deserved it, and second, that because Jesus took my punishment I therefore go free. There are many churches in which preaching the gospel means little more than repeating, explaining, and illustrating this statement. More than once, when I have preached or written about Jesus and his death in one of the many other ways the Bible explains it, I have been accused of not preaching the gospel.

Just to be clear, this theme (Jesus dying in my place) is indeed prominent in the Bible. Many people over the years have found that putting it this way addresses them sharply, stops them in their tracks, and opens before them a sense of the rescuing love and power of God coming to meet them with good news. My own earliest Christian memory, from when I was a small boy, is of being overwhelmed by the fact that Jesus had died for me. That is wonderful, foundational, and it must never be lost.

But there are serious difficulties with stating things in this brief and simple way. The Bible says a lot more about Jesus's death than simply that he died for our sins. How does the rest fit together? The Bible says a lot more about the gospel than this, too, as many passages indicate. So there is (a) more to Jesus's death than this, and (b) more to the gospel than Jesus's death. If we are to be biblical in our thinking (and most people who insist upon the gospel in the sense I just mentioned also claim to be biblical), then we must look more widely, without losing the centrality of "Jesus died in my place." In particular, we must be sure that whatever we say about the death of Jesus, it clearly and visibly belongs with the good news of the kingdom of God.

One particular problem follows from this. When we take this brief statement ("Jesus died for your sins") as the only real meaning of the gospel, we can easily distort it. Let me show you what I mean.

If you visit the classical sites in Greece, Turkey, North Africa, and the Middle East, you will find bits and pieces of carved stone that must at one time have been part of a much larger object. They might be from a statue, or a temple, or some great public monument. Anything like that in Northern Europe would, by now, be in a museum. But in the lands farther to the south and east, there are so many fragments lying around in the scrubland of ancient ruins that you would need many new museums to house them all. From time to time, the archaeologists discover something that they *do* want to put in a museum—say, the carved figure of a person who seems to be doing something important. But they want, quite rightly, to help people see this figure in the larger context where it originally belonged. They might make an educated guess that it had been part of a group of figures, perhaps on a long display panel designed to decorate the wall of a house, a government building, or a temple. They might then reconstruct an artificial framework within the museum so that we can see how the figure might have looked when surrounded by the others. Many museums have such reconstructions to help us glimpse how things looked originally, when the single figure was part of a much larger group.

Now suppose the people organizing the display in this particular museum take this figure, a beautiful small carved statue of a woman, and place it within a reconstructed procession. The procession is on its way to a temple to offer a sacrifice. That, after all, is a common theme in many ancient monuments. The designers of the museum display might construct a complete picture of several other people in the procession, together with one or two sacrificial animals led by the priests who were going to slaughter them. There might well be a temple in the background, perhaps even a god or goddess looking down on the scene, approving of it and waiting for the ritual to reach its climax. There are plenty of ancient scenes like that, so it all makes sense. It's a reasonable enough assumption. The beautiful woman appears to be at home in this setting. She is looking away to the right, toward the temple and the sacrifice about to be offered. It all seems to work.

But then another archaeologist, excavating close to where the original carving was found, discovers several large stone fragments that seem to belong together—and that have a gap into which the beautiful carved woman would fit exactly. Very carefully, they reassemble the fragments, and sure enough, they go together. The statue of the woman fits perfectly in the vacant space. But now we see that the people who reconstructed the earlier monument in the museum had guessed wrong. The woman is indeed taking part in a procession, but it is not going to a temple to offer a sacrifice. The procession is headed toward a very different kind of ceremony. A dashing young prince is going to be crowned king. The woman appears to be a member of his family, perhaps a sister. And though she is looking to the right, the procession as a whole is moving to the left. She is glancing back at her own little child, who has stepped out of the line to look at a bird on a bush. It is a touching human moment within a grand royal scene. There is no doubt that this, rather than the earlier reconstruction, is where the woman belongs.

I hope the point is clear. When we find a fragment of any-thing—a statue, a painting, a scrap from a musical composition—it is always possible to make an educated guess at the larger structure to which it may have belonged. Sometimes these guesses turn out to be exactly right. Sometimes they are nearly right but not quite. Sometimes—as with our beautiful carved statue—they are intel-ligent and interesting but interestingly wrong.

Something like this, I suggest, has happened with the central and vital statement that the Messiah died for our sins. For all sorts of reasons, this important statement of the key first moment in the good news has been treated as a fragment in search of a context. The Bible supplies a context for this, but in many traditions this context is ignored. Instead, like the well-meaning directors of the archaeological museum, people have put together a different con-text. It's the same statue but a different kind of procession.

How does this work out?

Most people who regard the statement that Jesus died in your place as the center of the gospel place this truth, this beautiful fragment, into a larger story that goes like this. There is a God, and this God is angry with humans because of their sin. This God has the right, the duty, and the desire to punish us all. If we did but know it, we are all heading for an eternal torment in hell. But this angry God has decided to vent his fury on someone else instead—someone who happens to be completely innocent.

Indeed, it is his very own son! His wrath is therefore quenched, and we no longer face that terrible destiny. All we have to do is to believe this story and we will be safe.

That is the reconstructed scene offered in many churches, sermons, and books. It is not completely wrong. But as it stands, it is deeply misleading. It distorts the very thing it is trying to frame. It takes the truth that Jesus died in your place and puts it in the wrong context. It does indeed make some sense there. But this is not the same sense that it would make if you put it in the right context. This, in anyone's account, is near the heart of what the early Christians meant by the good news. Since it is also, clearly, near the heart of what many Christians today understand by the good news, it is important that we sort this out.

There are two telltale signs that something has gone wrong. First, in the Bible the various statements about the death of Jesus in our place come within the double narrative of *creation* and *covenant*. *Creation* here is God the creator, the God to whom the whole world belongs and who longs to put that world right at last. *Covenant* (a kind of formal pledge): here is God calling the Israelites to be his people, undertaking to rescue them from slavery and bring them to the promised land, guiding them through trials and troubles all the way through their history to the sending of the Messiah. You can't ignore creation and covenant and expect the fragments that are left to make sense.

Second, the point of both these stories is that the God who masterminds both creation and covenant is a God of *love*—utter, self-giving, merciful, reconciling, healing, restorative love. You would never know this from listening to the story of the angry God who is determined to punish someone and just happens to pick on his own son. There is a famous verse in John's Gospel that says, "God so *loved* the world that he sent his only son." Not, please note, "God so *hated* the world." If we give the wrong impression at that point, we distort the whole picture.

Now, let's be clear. I would rather have someone walking around thinking, "Wow! Jesus died for my sins!" than thinking, "Forget this God-and-Jesus rubbish—let's get drunk and rob a bank." Better, by far, that someone should grasp the truth that "Jesus died in my place," even if it is within the wrong narrative. But that may store up trouble for later—later in your reading of the Bible or later in your understanding of Christian truth. Later, more worryingly still, in your inner heart and soul, as you continue to live with this sense of a God who is angry but who has (so we hope) been pacified. Later, too, if you are called to teach others about the Christian faith.

At this point someone might say, "But wait a minute! Surely Paul himself, in his famous letter to the Romans, begins by insisting that God is wrathful against sinners and goes on to explain that Jesus died in our place! Are you saying that's all wrong?" No, I'm not. But my point is that, precisely there in the opening chapters of Romans, Paul also does four other things, which set that picture in a very different context.

First he makes it clear that the wrath of God is the result of humans distorting his good creation—including human nature. The wrath of God is simply the shadow side of the love of God for his wonderful creation and his amazing human creatures. Like a great artist appalled at the way his paintings have been defaced by the very people who were supposed to be looking after them, God's implacable rejection of evil is the natural outflowing of his creative love. God's anger against evil is itself the determination to *put things right,* to get rid of the corrupt attitudes and behaviors that have spoiled his world and his human creatures. It is because God loves the glorious world he has made and is utterly determined to put everything right that he is utterly opposed to everything that spoils or destroys that creation, especially the human creatures who were supposed to be the linchpins of his plan for how that creation would flourish. That's why, as Paul's

argument progresses in this same letter, he frames its central passage not with God's *anger* but with his powerful, rescuing *love*
(Rom. 5:1–11; 8:31–39).

Many times, when people preach what they think is the gospel
from the letter to the Romans, you would never know that underneath the warning about wrath is the glorious truth of divine
love. A poet who had written a wonderful, long poem would be
horrified if someone came and tore pages out of it or crossed out
some of the best lines and scribbled in bits of doggerel instead. It
is because God loves the world he has made, and especially his
human creatures, that he hates everything that spoils, wrecks, or
defaces it. Paul emphasizes *creation*.

Second, Paul makes it clear that what has happened as a result
of Jesus is the fulfillment of God's ancient promises to Abraham
and his family (Rom. 4). God made the covenant with Abraham, and it is to fulfill that covenant that he has now sent Jesus.
Abraham, here and elsewhere in Paul, is not just an example of
someone who believed in God many years ago. Paul is reminding
his readers of the great procession, the story of God and Israel,
which through many twists and turns has prepared the way for
the coronation of Jesus—for Jesus to come as Messiah, as Israel's
rightful, long-awaited king.

Many times, when people preach what they think is the gospel from Romans, you would never think that the death of Jesus
means what it means because it is the fulfillment of these ancient
promises. God's promises give a shape and body to the whole
thing that is regularly missing in popular presentations of the gospel. Paul's vision of gospel is all about *covenant*.

After all, when Paul summarizes the gospel in 1 Corinthians
15, he says that the Messiah died for our sins "in accordance with
the Bible," and was raised from the dead "in accordance with the
Bible." As we saw earlier, that doesn't just mean, "I can find half
a dozen proof texts for all this." It means, "The entire scriptural

narrative is leading the eye to this point." Paul is situating Jesus
not in a narrative about an angry God who might just let us into
heaven after all but in a narrative about the God who, to renew
the creation, made covenant promises, and who has now kept
those promises.

Third, when we follow Paul's line of thought through to its climax in Romans 8, it becomes clear that the goal of God's rescue
operation, the main aim of Jesus coming and dying in the first
place, is *the restoration and transformation of all creation.* The slimmed-
down version of the gospel is regularly placed within a story in
which heaven is the goal—heaven, that is, imagined as a place
completely different from the present world, and indeed leaving
this present world out of consideration altogether. This version of
the gospel is often so thoroughly focused on heaven that anything
to do with the present creation is regarded as worldly, dangerous,
a distraction from the task of saving . . . but saving what? Well,
often it is saving souls. But there's nothing about souls in Romans
8. No mention of heaven, either, if it comes to that. It is all about
bodies: resurrection bodies, because that's what we will need in
the new creation, which will be *more* physical than the present
world, not less. (Why more? Because there will be no decay, no
death, no corruption. Imagine a physical world where everything
is solid and indestructible. Is that hard to imagine? That's because
we are so used to a world of decay and death that we allow decay
and death to state the terms, to tell us what we can and can't believe.)

Many times, when people preach the gospel from the letter to
the Romans, they entirely miss this passage about new creation.
As a result, they distort the entire message of the book. For Paul,
covenant led to *new creation.*

When we say, "Jesus died for our sins" within a message about
how to escape this nasty old world and go to heaven, it means one
thing. When we say, "Jesus died for our sins" within a message

about God the creator rescuing his creation from corruption, decay, and death, and rescuing us to be part of that, it means something significantly different.

Fourth, and finally, for Paul the story of the gospel *is much more like a coronation than a sacrifice*. The procession is going in the other direction. For starters, when Paul summarizes the gospel, he doesn't actually say "Jesus"; he says "the Messiah"—that is, the anointed king, the one who will sit on the throne of David. And when he summarizes the gospel again at the start of Romans, he doesn't emphasize the death of Jesus at all. "The good news," he says, is about "[God's] son, who was descended from David's seed in terms of flesh, and who was marked out powerfully as God's son in terms of the spirit of holiness by the resurrection of the dead" (Rom. 1:3-4). When Paul talks about the death of Jesus later in the letter, it is within *this* story: the story of the young prince who comes to be enthroned.

Many times, when people preach the gospel from Romans, they effectively start with 1:16–17, where Paul talks about the righteousness of God and salvation. That's fine in one sense. Those are great and central themes. But Romans begins at the beginning, and the beginning is about Jesus the Messiah. The prince on the way to his throne.

Yes, the story is also about his sacrifice. That's where my illustration of the two processions breaks down (as all illustrations eventually do). But the bigger picture, throughout Paul's letters, is about Jesus establishing his rule. His death is a vital and central part of how that is done. We cannot bypass it. We cannot downplay it. We cannot underemphasize it. But it makes the sense it makes within *this* picture: of the love of God, the covenant of God, the plan of God for the fulfillment of the whole of creation, not its abolition, and above all, the coronation of Jesus as the world's rightful king and lord. Many times, when people preach the gospel and talk of Jesus dying in our place, you would never

Buddhist, Allah?

guess at any of these things. And you would be left clinging to
a fragment of the biblical witness, supposing that the fragment
belonged in a quite different story.

What has happened? How have preachers and teachers allowed
these distortions to take place? That question requires a much
longer answer than is appropriate at the moment, but let me just
say this. To imagine a gospel that has forgotten about creation and
covenant; to imagine a gospel with an angry deity who is pacified only by the blood of an innocent victim; to imagine good
news that, instead of restoring and completing the work of the
world's creation, is prepared to throw away the world and take
some people ("souls") to a different location, namely a disembod-
ied heaven—this picture looks far more like a complicated form
of paganism than genuine biblical Christianity.

It is paganism (of a certain type), not Christianity, that treats
the created order as a prison from which we must escape rather
than a project its creator is determined to complete. It is paganism
(of almost any type), not biblical Christianity, that discounts the
story of God's covenant with Israel and treats it as a distraction, a
side issue, or simply an irrelevance. And it is certainly paganism
that imagines a malevolent, irascible deity determined to take out
his wrath on someone and eventually doing so on the one victim
who didn't deserve it.

Many Christians, and many non-Christians, too, have reacted
strongly to that kind of picture. That is hardly surprising. It is
attractive in some ways, but it is also repulsive. It is attractive because it offers a clear diagnosis of the human problem and a clear
remedy to match. You know exactly where you are with it. It is
repulsive because it seems to require that we set aside every shred
of moral value we have ever known and embrace the picture of a
terrifying and violent God.

Indeed, some who find it attractive may do so for the wrong
reasons. People who grew up with angry or violent fathers may

grasp this way of putting things only too well, and it will reinforce for them the idea that this is indeed what God is like.
(All fathers labor under the burden that our children are likely to *really?*
imagine God in our image.) People who are taught from an early
age that this story is the gospel may internalize that idea of God,
even if their own fathers were models of gentleness and kindness.

People who are repelled by this picture of God may well draw
the conclusion that this Christianity business isn't for them—or
even that this God business isn't for them. The sad thing is that
they usually don't realize that it never was the full biblical picture
in the first place. They then think to themselves that the whole
Bible, or the whole Christian faith, is simply unacceptable. That
is like someone who comes to a party but by mistake rings the
doorbell next door, to be greeted by anger and abuse. Startled,
they turn away, thinking the invitation must have been a trick.
Meanwhile, the party is going on in the right house . . . but they
missed it.

Those who teach this shrunken, misshapen version of the gospel are quite used to getting negative reactions. They have an
answer ready: this is the scandal of the cross. Paul, as we saw,
talks about that, too, mostly in 1 Corinthians and Galatians. But
they are making a mistake. Yes, the message of the cross is indeed
a scandal, something that causes people to draw back in horror.
In Paul's language, the word *scandal* meant "something that trips
people up." The message about Jesus's crucifixion caused people
to stumble. But that doesn't mean anything that causes people to
trip up must be the genuine article.

I remember someone pointing out to me when I was a teen-
ager that, while it was true that people might well dislike you for
being a good Christian, this didn't mean that, if people disliked
you, you were necessarily a good Christian. Perhaps you were
just being obnoxious. In the same way, just because people are
scandalized by a particular way of talking about Jesus's death, that

doesn't mean the preacher has got it right. The thing that's scandalizing people might be a distortion not only of the gospel but of the picture of God. What is putting people off might not be the good news but rather what seems to them, with some justification, to be bad news.

There, then, is the first problem we face, not least in the churches, in coming to grips with the good news in all its glory. I think this problem goes back at least to the Middle Ages, when, as many paintings from the period indicate, people were constantly being told that the point of the whole game was to go to heaven, and the problem was an angry God who didn't seem to want you to get there. The great Reformers in the sixteenth century tried to give new, biblical answers to these questions, but people were often left with the basic picture intact. And it is the basic picture that constitutes the problem.

The Competing Gospels of Rationalism and Romanticism

The second problem has infected both the church and the world for the last two or three hundred years at least. Again, this is not the place to explain how all the complicated ideas in modern European and American thought came about and bounced off one another, producing the worldviews many hold today. But we can at least say this.

The churches, having long believed that the point of everything was to go to heaven, were vulnerable to a new cultural movement. Picking up from certain strands of thought in the ancient world, many thinkers in the eighteenth century (famous names come to mind, such as Rousseau in France or Jefferson in America) embraced a philosophy in which God and the world were split apart. God was pushed upstairs like a dysfunctional and embarrassing elderly relative. People who still felt affection for him were welcome to go and visit him, in private prayer and Sunday worship. People who still believed he mattered would hope to be with him forever after their death. *But he had nothing to say about how to run the downstairs world.* Jesus's prayer that God's kingdom would come "on earth as in heaven" was either forgotten or reinterpreted. Since that was, in fact, a basic element of *his* good news, this change has meant that the understanding of this phrase has also changed. Private piety in the present, heaven in the future (if you were lucky, or if you believed the right doctrines): that was Christianity. That was the good news. It had nothing much to do with what people usually call the real world.

Most Western churches have gone along for the ride. In fact, many are deeply shocked if you suggest that when Jesus said that all authority in heaven *and on earth* had been given to him (Matt. 28:18), he meant what he said and we should work it out in practice. Many neither believe nor teach that when Jesus and his first followers spoke about good news, they meant that something had *happened* (or was happening) as a result of which the world had become a different place, and that they should be working to make it so. But that's what Jesus and his early followers meant. We should notice, though, that most people today have not actually rejected that idea. They simply haven't thought about it, because nobody has ever put it to them like that.

The danger, then, is that if someone *does* start talking about the good news of God's kingdom coming on earth as in heaven, those who are comfortable with things as they are now will reject the notion as being worldly and unspiritual. At the same time, those who are keen to see social and political change may well seize the idea of God's kingdom just a bit too eagerly, hoping that this kingdom will produce, at last, whatever kind of social or political reform they happen to want. (Jesus faced that problem, too.) Both groups, I suspect, need to be confronted with the puzzle we noted earlier: the good news is foolishness to some and scandal to others. If we think it's just what we want, that probably shows we didn't get the point.

What happened over the last four centuries was something like this. Back in the time of Reformers like Luther and Calvin, and in the days of Shakespeare half a century later, people still had a sense that the world was a complex but complete system. The universe was God-given, and it all fitted together, even if we mortals couldn't always see exactly how. But that complete, complex world was pulled apart by the Enlightenment. For all sorts of reasons in the eighteenth century—partly scientific, partly political, but particularly philosophical—people began to think of the world as being divided in two. God does the spiritual bits, and we do the worldly bits—making money, gaining power, conquering territory, and things like that. So people who still wanted to embrace something called Christianity were left purely with the so-called spiritual part, failing to realize that, in the Bible at least, all creation belongs to God, and he intends to flood it with his love and justice "as the waters cover the sea" (Isa. 11:9). This is partly why some Christians today explain the gospel in terms of people having fellowship with God, or something like that. They can make sense of this within the split-level world. The rest of the older vision has been screened out.

One result is that some key words have changed meaning. People used to talk about the "supernatural" world as a way of reminding one another that creation is multidimensional. Whether, following one poet, you think of glimpsing eternity in a grain of sand or, with another, you say that the world is "charged with the grandeur of God," you are drawing attention to something that used to be called supernatural, in the sense of another dimension of present reality. But with the big split that came about through eighteenth-century thought (where we humans decided we would run the world and that God, if there was a God, could be safely packed off upstairs to heaven, where people could go and visit him if they wished), the word *supernatural* was also sent upstairs. Almost by definition, it now means "something that normally has no business in our downstairs world but might show up here from time to time." The very word *supernatural* has become a way of confirming that the world is split in two.

Part of the good news in our own culture is that this split-level world doesn't have the last word. There is an integrated worldview, and it's available right now. The trouble is that *both* the secularists *and* the fundamentalists are committed to not noticing it. The secularist lives downstairs and has locked the door at the bottom of those stairs. The fundamentalist lives upstairs, though he constantly shouts down the stairs to tell people they should be coming up to join him.

In this way, Western Christianity has taken a series of small but significant steps away from the full biblical picture, especially from the idea of good news—the idea that something happened in the first century as a result of which everything is different. Because Western Protestants in particular have always claimed to be biblical, they haven't noticed how far they've drifted from that first-century way of seeing things. There is thus an ever-increasing gap between those who understand—and explore—the gloriously many-sided world of the Bible and those who have taken one or two ideas from it, puffed them up into entire systems, and trumpeted them all the way down the street. This is part of the reason why understanding the original and quite simple good news is harder today than it ought to be.

There are two further wrinkles in this picture. Both have had a considerable impact on how people in our day, particularly in the churches, understand the message *of* Jesus and the message *about* Jesus. Educationalists used to talk about the three *R*s: Reading, wRiting, and aRrithmetic. Here are two other *R*s that have radically affected the understanding of the Christian good news:

Rationalism and Romanticism. Both inside the church and outside it, these two movements have left their mark, reinforcing the
basic problem of the split-level universe.

Again, we must cut corners and go straight to the heart of it.
Rationalism can refer to various philosophical theories, particularly
the idea (prominent in the eighteenth century) that we humans
know things primarily by reason rather than through our senses.
But it can also refer to the belief that knowledge about God and
Christian truth can come through reason alongside, or even in
place of, revelation (that is, scripture and the Spirit-led teaching
of the church). Both these forms of rationalism can lead to, or at
least accompany, a deep skepticism about God, or the Bible, or
Jesus, or theology in general.

Whatever position one takes on such matters, however, one of
the legacies of eighteenth-century rationalism, even among devout Christians who resist its skeptical side, has been a concentra-
tion on reasoned-out propositions. For many people, believing
in God or believing in heaven and hell or believing in Jesus can
be reduced to believing in propositions such as "There is a God"
or "Jesus died for my sins" or "Jesus truly rose from the dead."
The whole focus then shifts—ironically, of course—away from
the events to which those propositions refer to *the propositions themselves.*
The church, faced with rationalist skepticism, has resorted to rationalist apologetics, the attempt to prove from first principles the
truth of Christianity. In doing so, the church always runs the risk
of capitulating at a deeper level to the idea that the Christian faith
is not after all about events that took place in the first century but
about the true ideas that those events might or might not reveal.
In fact, its arguments often subtly reinforce the split-level world.
What matters is abstract truth, a kind of upstairs reality, rather
than the downstairs reality of God's kingdom arriving on earth
as in heaven.

Let me be clear. Reason, properly understood, is certainly an ally of the Christian faith—precisely because that faith highlights the glorious renewal of all human life, including human thought, as a vital element in the Creator's plan. Reasonable, thought-out, clearly displayed exposition of every aspect of Christian faith has always been an important part of the overall life and witness of the church. There is, however, a danger, which many modern movements (particularly fundamentalism) have not escaped, that we (a) express all our beliefs in apparently crisp, sharp propositions, then (b) insist that true Christianity means believing exactly these propositions, and finally (c) insist that only such belief counts as true, justifying faith, such as would qualify one for "going to heaven." This is a great danger, and it's no wonder that many devout Christians in other traditions look upon it as an unpleasant caricature.

The opposite problem comes with the natural reaction to rationalism: romanticism. This, too, means different things to different people and comes to expression in such varied spheres as music, art, and literature, as well as philosophy. At the center, though, it represents a rejection of cold rationalism and the embrace, instead, of a warm, life-affirming, intuitive awareness of the world, including the possibility of mystical experience and insight. Thus while the rationalistic Christian apologist says, "But I can prove it!" the romantic says, "Trust me, you'll find your heart strangely warmed!" The appeal to *experience* and *feeling* thus appears to trump everything. In particular, it appears to take precedence over any sense that what matters is the events that took place, as unique and world-changing moments, in the first century.

Experience and feeling are central parts of normal Christian life. Our emotions swing wildly this way and that, according to the weather, our relationships, our diet, and a thousand other things. But Christians from the beginning have been aware of the deeply consoling and challenging presence of one whom they recognize as the living Lord himself, Jesus, and through him, the unimaginable but still knowable God whom Jesus called Father. This is not, of itself, a prerogative of modern "romantic" Christians. But the romanticism of the last two centuries has provided many apparently natural ways in which Christians with a particular concern for the interior and experiential side of the faith have been able to express that concern. This, too, contains a great danger, namely the privileging of such experience, whether through the deep emotions stirred up by wonderful liturgy and music, the passionate excitement of charismatic worship, or similar phenomena. What happens when the excitement dies down? As wise romantic thinkers know, the truly life-changing experience comes when experience is the accidental by-product of something else. Whipping up emotion for its own sake, then calling that emotion faith and insisting that such faith is the key to eternal life is just as much a caricature as rationalism is.

The problem with both rationalism and romanticism is that they divert attention from the central message of the gospel. They try to get the fruits (Christianity does make sense; Christianity does involve the personal experience of God's presence and love) without the roots (Christianity is about something that *happened,* which constitutes the good news). Both movements, then, not only in their non-Christian forms but specifically in the way they have encouraged Christians to embrace them, have led many in the church far away from the central emphasis of the good news. The good news is not simply, "Look, I can prove these abstract truths" nor yet "Your heart can be filled with joy" but "The Messiah died for our sins in accordance with the Bible and was raised on the third day in accordance with the Bible." Something has *happened* that has made all the difference. Modern Western culture, with its split-level universe, finds this difficult to accommodate, and the churches have consequently toned down their idea of the good news. As a result, the message both of Paul and of Jesus (chapters 2 and 3 above) has been hard to hear, let alone to grasp.

There is one more feature of our modern cultural landscape that has made it supremely difficult to understand the original good news.

The Competing Gospel of the Modern World

The first problem, we recall, is that the church has colluded with the legacy of the Middle Ages, proposing going to heaven as the ultimate goal and an angry God as the problem to get around. The second is that modern culture has operated with a split-level universe, and in attempting to cope with this, the church has often merely colluded with it. The third, and I think the greatest, problem standing in the way of any understanding of what the first good news was actually about is found in a huge claim that dominates Western culture to this day. This is the belief that world history turned a vital and defining corner not with anything that happened in the first century but with something that happened in the eighteenth.

Ever since the middle of that century, people in the Western world—Europe, America, and their various satellites—have said to themselves and to one another that a great change came over the world with the arrival of new science and technology. We have entered the modern period. The world is now a different place.

So indeed it is. Compare the remarkably settled life of almost all people in the world up to that point with the opportunities for travel provided by railways, then by cars, and then by airplanes, and you'll see that the change has been extraordinary. Compare what happens to seriously sick people now with what happened three hundred years ago. Modern anesthetics, penicillin, research into DNA, and a thousand other things have made an enormous difference. Compare the life expectancy of many in today's world with what it was even two hundred years ago. The world is indeed, in several senses, a different place from what it was. Many of those changes have brought a great sigh of relief. They have allowed millions to enjoy a longer and happier life than anyone would have thought possible in days gone by.

But this sense of a modern revolution has now gone way beyond the boundaries of new science and technology, new transport and medicine. A great many people believe that prior to the modern world everything was shrouded in ignorance and superstition. Without modern science, people didn't really know what the world was like. Without our newly enlightened understanding, they thought that the world was flat or the moon was made of green cheese or there were fairies at the bottom of the garden or there was an old man up in the sky called God who would throw you into hell unless you smartened up. Whereas we, of course, now know better. We have escaped the primitive slavery of such views. We are liberated; we are progressive. We know that the world is now advancing into its new age of freedom, the freedom to do what we like without fear of the old man upstairs.

Freedom and equality—these were slogans of the French Revolution in the late eighteenth century, and they still serve as the marching song of the modern enlightened mood to this day. (The third French slogan, brotherhood, is a bit harder, because we find ourselves locked in a struggle with people who don't see the world the way we do—which is, of course, what the French revolutionaries themselves discovered, though that is another story.) These slogans condition, in particular, the way people talk, not least in the media, which reinforces this viewpoint hour by hour and minute by minute. Whenever you hear someone say, "Now that we live in the twenty-first century . . ." or "In this day and age you would expect . . . ," you are hearing the Enlightenment, and it's assumed we have all signed on. Whenever people refer to a moral belief that almost everyone endorsed until twenty or thirty years ago as "stone age morality," they are appealing (with gross exaggeration) to chronological snobbery. Now that *we* have modern science and technology, we know that everything *they* believed, back in the dark ages or whenever, was just superstitious ignorance.

This narrative, about a dark past, a sudden illumination, and a bright future, has been applied particularly to political systems. Modern Western democracies look back in some sense to the Magna Carta of 1215. But they really took shape in the late eighteenth century. It has been widely assumed that this was a world-changing moment, like the invention of the wheel or the discovery of penicillin. Now we had discovered, along with modern science, how to run our countries! In particular, we had eliminated tyranny. We were self-determining. This was how things should be done. One of the reasons that modern Western powers have been so inept in reacting to events in other parts of the world is that we have all assumed that life really is that easy: here is a tyrant; get rid of him (it's usually a "him"), and liberal democracy will spring up automatically.

Many people today have this narrative in their heads. This is the problem. Millions of people in the modern Western world take it for granted that *the great defining turning point in human history happened with the rise of the modern Western world.* (Putting it like this shows just how self-centered and self-serving this belief has been.) If you look at the world that way, you are bound to see everything else reorganized around that central point. You will inevitably see some of what went before as superstition that is now out of date. You may, if you're feeling generous, see some earlier people and movements as forerunners of the brave new modern world. Many people have co-opted Jesus in that way: he was really a modern libertarian, born at the wrong time! What you will never be able to do is imagine that the great turning point in human history occurred when Jesus of Nazareth died as the would-be king of the Jews and was raised again three days later.

Since that is the center of the early Christian good news, anyone who holds the modern Western view will inevitably misunderstand it. Whatever you say about Jesus, you will fit him into the wrong categories. You will transform him into the teacher of a religion or perhaps a morality. (I heard someone on the television only last night speaking of the parables as containing Jesus's moral teaching.) Or you will fit him into the upstairs-downstairs world: he came from up above to rescue us from our plight down here and take us back with him. The idea of world history turning its great corner in the eighteenth century was, of course, a key part of an essentially secularizing movement. But many churches have colluded with this notion.

This third problem, then, can be put quite starkly. We can happily grant that in all sorts of ways the scientific and technological advances of the eighteenth century were epoch-making, and that in some respects the political transformations of the time were also dramatic and world changing. But to claim them as *the* single and all-important turning point in human history is to come into direct conflict with the Christian claim.

The early Christians, following from Jesus's announcement, declared the good news that through his death and resurrection the kingdom he announced had been launched. That was the ultimate turning point of history. The modern world has been taught, and believes at a deep level, that the eighteenth-century Enlightenment was the ultimate turning point.

We can't both be right.

This chapter has been long and complex, but vital, too, if we are to understand why the good news has been so difficult not

only for non-Christians to understand but for Christians to articulate and live by. As Paul found the gospel to be a scandal to some
and foolishness to others, attempts to reproduce his message in
the modern Western world have met with sneers and puzzlement,
not just of individuals but of an entire culture. For that reason,
and because of the long legacy of the Western world all the way
back at least to the Middle Ages, both the church and the world
have found it easier to make subtle adjustments to the message.

In that process, something essential to the message has been
lost. For Jesus himself, and for interpreters like Paul, the good
news was about something that was *happening* right then, through
Jesus himself and his death and resurrection. But this idea of an
event has proved difficult to fit into later worldviews, including
would-be Christian worldviews.

All this leads to one obvious question. If Jesus or Paul or anyone else really supposed that those events in the Middle East in
the first century AD were the fulcrum around which world history would turn, is this not manifest nonsense? Surely the world
rumbled on just as before. If anything really changed, wasn't it
simply the religious consciousness of Jesus's followers? Doesn't
that reinforce the idea that the good news was about simply opening up a spiritual or religious option for those who wanted that
kind of thing, not about a whole new world?

That perfectly appropriate question points to the next chapter.
As we recall, the way news works has to do not with one moment but with the long-term consequences of that moment. Not
simply with the victory of Octavian over Antony at the battle of
Actium, but with Octavian's return to Rome two years later. Not
simply with the victory of Jesus over the powers of evil, but with
his return in triumph. Good news about the past, as we saw, is
also good news about the future.

But what is this future? And why has this, too, been so hard for
people in our own day, Christian or not, to grasp?

It seems the interpretation of the bible leads people to understand or imagine so differently.

5

Rethinking Heaven

IF JESUS'S FIRST followers spoke about the good news of what *had* just happened, what did they think *would* happen in the future as a result? Here we face a major problem. For many generations in the modern church, followers of Jesus in many parts of the world have thought that the future event, the good news about what *was still to happen,* consisted of two things.

No First, Jesus was going to take us to be with him in heaven. There are different ways people have imagined this happening, but the message is still the same. Somehow, the good news in the past (what Jesus did two thousand years ago) points forward to one particular piece of good news about the future (he will take us to heaven). This completes the new relationship with God that is for many the sole focus of the good news. *And this is seriously misleading.*

No Second, Jesus would come back again. There are also different ways this has been expressed. Various Bible passages, some of them complex, speak about this future event, often in dramatic first-century picture language that is difficult to decode today.

There is no doubt that the first Christians did indeed speak of Jesus returning. But what exactly that meant and how we should grasp it today have often posed a problem. Many Western Christians in our own day have quietly abandoned the belief altogether, preferring to see such language as a bit of ancient mythology we can do without today.

Part of the reason is that some other Christians, especially within the split-level world I spoke of, have put these two expectations together and made something quite different out of them. For such people, the overarching point is to get to heaven. Whether they get there immediately after they die or whether Jesus comes back to take them to heaven with him, that's what they think it's all about. Elaborate theories about the second coming have been developed in which the whole point is that Jesus will come back, not to stay on this earth to transform and renew it, but to take his people away.

But this misses the whole point.

Once we understand the original good news, the news about something that *happened* in the events concerning Jesus, we also understand that the good news about the future cannot be about leaving earth and going to heaven. It must have something to do with heaven and earth coming together. Something to do with creation itself being renewed and restored.

This is a major theme of the Bible, and as I hinted earlier, it is screened right out in much modern Christian understanding. (I have written about this at considerably more length in *Surprised by Hope* [2008].) This, too, is a result of the split-level philosophy: Why bother about earth down here if what matters is going to heaven up there?

Let us say it again: the final vision of the Christian gospel—the goal it holds out before us—is *not* going to heaven when you die. The Bible says remarkably little about what happens to people, even to God's people, after they die—at least, *immediately* after they die. Eventually—ah, that's another story. The Bible, especially the New Testament, is very interested in what happens eventually. That is because the Bible, and the good news at its heart, are about *the rescue and renewal of the whole creation.* And if God will, in the end, transform the whole created order, flooding it with his presence and glory—and that is what we are promised—then what matters for us is not where we will be in the meantime but how we will get to share in that new world.

The last scene in the Bible (the book of Revelation, chapters 21 and 22) is not about saved souls going up to heaven. It is about the new Jerusalem coming down from heaven to earth, creating the new heaven and new earth, which are *one and the same place.* That is why Jesus taught his followers to pray, "Your kingdom come, your will be done, *on earth as in heaven.*" So if the good news about the *past* has to do with something Jesus did back then, the good news about the *future* has to do with something Jesus is going to do when he returns. He will transform the whole world and fill it with his justice, his joy, and his love. That is indeed good news.

So, like someone in Rome celebrating the victory of Octavian and looking forward to his enthronement when he returned to the capital, Jesus's followers also discovered good news about their present lives. They could begin, right then, to live in the light of this double good news about Jesus's initial achievement and future reign.

Like everything else in early Christian belief, this is rooted in the much older scriptures of Israel. Think of the vision of the prophet Isaiah, a vision of creation put right at last, of violence abolished and the world at peace. This is a vision—poetic, no doubt, but a signpost to a reality even greater, out beyond the reach of mere words—of what will happen when God puts everything right. The way he will do it is by setting the coming king ("a shoot from the stock of Jesse" or "the root of Jesse," Jesse being the father of King David) in charge of it all:

Father of King David. [handwritten annotation]

A shoot shall come out from the stock of Jesse,
    and a branch shall grow out of his roots.
The spirit of YHWH shall rest on him,
    the spirit of wisdom and understanding,
    the spirit of counsel and might,
the spirit of knowledge and the fear of YHWH.
    His delight shall be in the fear of YHWH.
He shall not judge by what his eyes see,
    or decide by what his ears hear;
but with righteousness he shall judge the poor,
    and decide with equity for the meek of the earth;
He shall strike the earth with the rod of his mouth,
    and with the breath of his lips he shall kill the wicked.
Righteousness shall be the belt around his waist,
    and faithfulness the belt around his loins.
The wolf shall live with the lamb,
    the leopard shall lie down with the kid,
the calf and the lion and the fatling together,
    and a little child shall lead them.
The cow and the bear shall graze,
    their young shall lie down together;
    and the lion shall eat straw like the ox.
The nursing child shall play over the hole of the asp,
    and the weaned child shall put its hand on the adder's den.
They will not hurt or destroy
    on all my holy mountain;
for the earth will be full of the knowledge of YHWH
    As the waters cover the sea.

On that day the root of Jesse shall stand as a signal to the peoples; the nations shall enquire of him, and his dwelling shall be glorious. (Isa. 11:1–10)

Or think, in a similar vein, of the glorious vision of some of the Psalms:

> *Let the heavens be glad, and let the earth rejoice;*
> *let the sea roar, and all that fills it;*
> *let the field exult, and everything in it.*
> *Then shall all the trees of the forest sing for joy,*
> *before the LORD, for he is coming,*
> *for he is coming to judge the earth.*
> *He will judge the world with righteousness,*
> *and the peoples with his truth.* (Ps. 96:11–13)

This is the hope we also find in many passages in the New Testament. In the letter to the Ephesians, for instance, Paul declares that God's ultimate plan was "to sum up the whole cosmos in the king [i.e., in Jesus, the Davidic Messiah]—yes, everything in heaven and on earth" (Eph. 1:10). That single verse points to the longer expositions of the same point in 1 Corinthians 15 and above all Romans 8, both of which we glanced at in chapter 2. The same point emerges in the remarkable poem in the letter to the Colossians, chapter 1, which celebrates the creation of the entire world and everything in it "in him . . . through him and for him" (1:16), and goes on to declare that "in him" (that is, again, in Jesus the Messiah) everything on the earth and in the heavens would be reconciled to God. The New Testament is not interested in an ultimate hope that leaves earth out of consideration. That is why popular talk about heaven is so misleading. What matters is new heaven and new earth.

From long experience of talking with people about these things, I know that at least two people in my audience will be putting their hands up with questions right now. Both have Bible verses that seem to contradict what I just said.

The first person quotes John 18:36: "My kingdom is not of this world." That, however, is the King James translation, and it doesn't catch the flavor of the original. It sounds to us as though Jesus is talking about a nonworldly kingdom, which modern Western Christians automatically assume means a heavenly one, one to which God's people go when they die, away from this world altogether. But the original points in a different direction. What Jesus said was, "My kingdom isn't the sort that grows in this world." It isn't worldly in its *origin* or in its *character*. It is not *from* this world; it doesn't originate here, but it certainly is *for* this world. Jesus is launching, as we saw earlier, *a different kind of kingdom,* based on *a different kind of power.* But there's no point launching this kingdom in heaven, away from earth. Heaven works like that already. What matters is getting this sort of kingdom launched on earth. That's what the good news is all about.

The second person quotes Philippians 3:20: "We are citizens of heaven." This time the speaker is using the New English Bible, and my own translation agrees with it. That is what the verse says and means. But once again we misunderstand what is going on. The logic of citizenship in the ancient world, certainly the Roman citizenship of which many in Philippi would be proud possessors, didn't work the way we imagine. We hear, "We are citizens of heaven," and we think, "Yes, heaven is where we really belong, and that's where we will go when we die." But that isn't what Paul says, and it isn't how citizenship worked in his world. The whole reason for having colonies like Philippi in the first place was that there were too many old soldiers who had fought in the civil wars. Rome was overcrowded and needed to import food. The last thing Rome wanted was thousands more hungry mouths coming home—especially when the mouths belonged to trained killers, used to getting things done through violence. The point about Philippi being a colony of Rome was not that the citizens would go back to Rome one day, but that (so it was hoped) they would bring the benefits of Roman civilization to Philippi.

That, after all, is how Paul expands the image. "We are citizens of heaven, you see," he writes, "and we're eagerly waiting for the savior, the Lord, King Jesus, who is going to come from there" (Phil. 3:20). It isn't that *we* are going off to the capital city to join the king; *he* is going to come *from* there to transform our lives here. "He's going to do this by the power which makes him able to bring everything into line under his authority," Paul concludes (3:21). Jesus will come *from* heaven to transform the whole of creation— and to transform us at the same time. "Our present body is a shabby old thing, but he's going to transform it so that it's just like his glorious body" (3:21). That is the hope. Not that we leave this world but that Jesus returns and transforms it, and us with it.

Once we grasp this picture, many things come into focus, helping us see how the good news of what *happened* back in the first century is organically related to the good news of what *will happen* when Jesus returns. The Gospel stories of Jesus's resurrection, especially the account in John's Gospel, are not told in order to say, "There, that proves there really is a life after death" or "There, that proves Jesus was divine." There *is* a life beyond the grave, and Jesus really *does* embody the personal presence of the living God, but that isn't the main point. The main point is that *the new creation has begun,* and this beginning points to the ultimate conclusion, the consummation of it all.

This means that the early Christians were able to retrieve, and to use with a new sharp focus, all those ancient biblical promises about Israel's God coming back to his people to overthrow their masters, set them free, and come to live in their midst. For the early Christians, the new exodus *had* happened in Jesus, ahead of time, as it were. The new exodus *would* therefore happen when death itself was defeated and God was "all in all."

We need to be very clear about this, because so many pressures are pushing the other way. *God made this world of space, time, and matter; he loves it, and he is going to renew it.* The new creation will be what we would call *physical,* though that word doesn't say half enough. *Physical* for us means, mostly, stuff that we can touch and see, but also stuff that we can chop down or cut up, or burn or smash—stuff that, left to itself, will mostly rot and decay all by itself. God's new world, it seems, will be of a completely different kind. The only language we have for it is picture language, but if Paul means what he says—that "creation itself would be freed from its slavery to decay, to enjoy the freedom that comes when God's children are glorified" (Rom. 8:21)—then we must imagine the future world as a more solid, more permanent, more altogether glorious place than this present one. Imagine the most beautiful sunset you have ever seen, set in the most beautiful scenery. Imagine the most stunning birdsong you have ever heard. Imagine the most delicate flower, the most spectacular mountain. These are all just long-range signposts pointing to the unimaginable beauty of the new creation.

And part of the good news is that we will be there ourselves, with bodies to match. So many preachers, asked to talk about the good news, speak of a heaven that, as some cynics have said, will involve us simply lying around all day listening to people playing harps. Well, in God's new creation it is clear that all we do will be bathed in worship. If God is personally present, as we are promised, then of course we will respond appropriately. But we will be *more truly human*—more fully ourselves, in every sense. God made humans to reflect his glory, his love, his wisdom into the world, and in the new creation God will not revoke this vocation. He will gloriously fulfill it. We will become *more* human, not less. If, in the present, we have been given tasks to do, vocations to pursue, the ability to delight in music and love and light and laughter, then it would be strange if, in the new creation, none of this mattered anymore.

But speculating about the precise details of the resurrection life within the new creation is not the point at the moment.

The point is that the meaning of the good news changes radically depending on whether you think it means, "Here's how you leave this universe and go somewhere else called heaven," or whether you think it means, "Here's how God is remaking the entire creation and offering you a new bodily life within that." If we are promised new heaven and new earth, a whole new universe in which God's space and our space are brought together once and for all—and that's what the New Testament writers say again and again—then the good news is news about, and news *for,* the whole of creation, not just a few humans who get the magic password that lets them off the hook and into heaven after all.

Saving the World

But how does the good news of the death and resurrection of Jesus and the good news that this was for our sins and in accordance with the scriptures turn out to be the good news of the new creation? How are these things joined together? The answer is simple—and revolutionary. *God wants to put humans right to put the world right.* And the good news is that this, too, has been accomplished through Jesus.

Here again popular Christian traditions and popular Christian preaching have shrunk the underlying message of the New Testament. We all imagined the point to be simply that humans needed rescuing and God did this through Jesus. We imagined the problem to be that we were out of touch with God and we needed to reestablish a relationship with him. Well, that is all true, but it's not the whole truth. We forgot what humans (so to speak) were there for in the first place. God made humans so that he could look after his world *through* this particular creature. His intention was to bring his creation forward from its beginnings

to be the glorious place he always intended and to do so through
this human family.

That is one part of what it means to be in the image of God.
God is not an object in the world, but he wanted from the first
to be present and active in his world, so he created humans to
be the means and mode of that presence and that activity. That
is why human rebellion against the Creator's intentions was so
disastrous—not just for the humans but for the whole of creation.

Those who know the story of Genesis will know that when
the first humans rebelled, they were told that the earth would
henceforth be harder for them to work. It would produce sharp,
unpleasant weeds—thorns and thistles. We have been inclined, I
think, to see this as a problem simply for the humans: life is going
to be tough. And so it is. But this is also a problem for the earth itself. Creation was supposed to be brought to flourishing harmony,
to a fruitful fulfillment, through the work of humans. So creation
itself is frustrated, all because the humans got it wrong. The problem is not "Oh dear, humans sinned, so they will now go to hell."
The problem is "Humans sinned, so the whole creation will fail
to attain its proper goal." Perhaps that failure, if not dealt with, is
part of what we should mean by hell.

The good news, therefore, is that when humans are put right,
the project can get back on track. Not all at once, of course, just
as we humans are not put right completely and forever at a stroke.
But this is the goal.

All this brings us back to our earlier themes of coronation, covenant, and creation. In the New Testament, Jesus announces that
God is becoming king. He is enthroned—that's how the Gospel
writers see it—as, on the cross, he completes his work of covenant
renewal, the forgiveness of sins. And all this is so that humans thus
rescued from their sins can resume their proper work as image
bearers. Unless the good news contains this as a major strand, it is
selling itself short. To say "Jesus died for your sins" ought to lead

at once to "so you can freely pick up your role as a truly human being and discover your particular vocation within God's purposes for his world."

There are, sadly, some people for whom the good news, as they have been taught it, leaves them with a vacuum. Now that I've believed this good news, they think—now that I know I will go to heaven one day—what is there to do in the meantime? Those who find themselves thinking that ought to go back to whoever taught them the good news and, metaphorically speaking, demand their money back. You've only been given one part of the gospel. The good news is bigger, better, fuller than you ever imagined.

Resurrection as the Beginning of a New World

How do we know all this? How *can* we know all this? How is all this not simply a pious dream, a fantasy, a utopia that we all enjoy but know is a mirage? The answer is simple. *Jesus was raised from the dead.* This is, of course, the second half of the classic summary of the gospel. Following "The Messiah died for our sins in accordance with the scriptures," we find "and he was buried, and he was raised from the dead on the third day in accordance with the scriptures." The good news about the *future* is utterly dependent on the good news about the *past*. Christian life is shaped by both.

The resurrection of Jesus is *the launching of God's new world.* You can tell because of the way the story is told, particularly in John's Gospel. John tells the story in such a way as to echo themes both in the Genesis creation story and in his own prologue, which itself echoes that story.

But the point goes far beyond simple biblical allusions. The resurrection is presented, together with Jesus's crucifixion, as the climax of the entire biblical narrative.

yes.

God made the world as a *project:* the garden of Eden was the start of something, not a small world in which Adam and Eve might live a languid life like figures in a private tableau. Their failure meant that the project was aborted, or at least radically corrupted and put on hold. But with Jesus—precisely with Jesus as the true king, the Messiah—the project has now been restarted. This is partly because, as some early Christians discerned, the Psalms spoke of the "son of man" who would inherit the role marked out for Adam and Eve in Genesis 1, looking after the garden and the animals on God's behalf. That is true, but it's not the whole truth.

The whole truth is that *Jesus himself, in his risen physical body, is the beginning of God's new creation.* He not only presides over that new creation; he *is* that new creation, in person. Everything about the larger Christian hope follows from this. "He is the start of it all," writes Paul, "firstborn from realms of the dead; so in all things he might be chief" (Col. 1:18). This is where the good news provides the launching pad, not for people to go to heaven but for people to discover that *God's new world has begun, and we can be part of it.* Welcome to the full meaning of the good news.

I hope it is now clear why the resurrection of Jesus is so central and vital—as Paul insists again and again, especially in 1 Corinthians 15:17. "If the Messiah wasn't raised," he writes, "your faith is pointless, and you are still in your sins." If the Messiah is not raised, the covenant is not renewed, creation is not renewed, and . . . he is not even the Messiah in the first place. The resurrection is the sign that the verdict of the courts has been reversed. The Jewish court tried Jesus for blasphemy and found him guilty; the resurrection declared that he really was God's son. Pilate's court tried him for being a would-be rebel leader, and though Pilate didn't really find Jesus guilty, he handed him over on that charge. The resurrection declared that Jesus was not the ordinary sort of political king, a rebel leader, that some had supposed. He was the leader of a far larger, more radical revolution than anyone had ever supposed. He was inaugurating a whole new world, a new creation, a new way of being human. He was forging a way into a new cosmos, a new era, a form of existence hinted at all along but never before unveiled. Here it is, he was saying. This is the new creation you've been waiting for. It is open for business. Come and join in.

All this shows, if further proof were needed, that the cross and resurrection are closely bound together in the full meaning of the gospel. It is inconceivable that the new creation could begin if sin, evil, corruption, decay, and death still had the power to thwart it. God would not begin for a second time something that could be radically derailed by human pride, rebellion, idolatry, or sin. God would not launch this new, immortal creation in a world where death still held everything in its icy grip. The resurrection makes sense because the victory was won on the cross. The two events go together at every level. And they form the foundation for the eventual new creation.

The resurrection thus completes Jesus's coronation as Messiah, the true king and lord. It also completes the narrative of the *covenant*. It announces that the project God began with the calling of Abraham has reached its fruition. This could be a long story, but we will here make it a short one. The story of Israel, at so many points, had seemed to go down into the valley of the shadow of death, only to have God rescue it and bring it out again. That was what happened with the exodus. It happened again and again in the dark years under the judges. It happened on a grand scale in the exile in Babylon. And it was during that period that the prophet Ezekiel spoke of return from exile in terms of bodily resurrection. In his vision of the "valley of the dry bones," he had seen long-dead bones come together into skeletons, acquire flesh and sinews, and finally breathe (see Ezek. 37). This, he declared, showed the restoration of God's people after their exile. God would do a new thing.

The early church went back to that picture in Ezekiel again and again when reflecting on the promise of future resurrection that still stood before the church. But Jesus's resurrection declares that *with this event, the exile is truly over.* Sins have been forgiven; the dark powers that stand behind all enslaving political authorities have been defeated; God's people are rescued from their long, sad sojourn under the rule of the pagans. Now they will live instead under the rule of the Messiah—the Messiah who has brought about the return from death of God's people. *The people of God die and are raised in the Messiah*: that is the meaning Paul, the first to write about the gospel, makes clear in passage after passage. If Jesus is crowned as king, then he represents his people, and in him the covenant is at last fulfilled. God has done what he promised.

If this is so, then, as we have said, the resurrection of Jesus means the launching of the new creation. Imagine that picture of exile and restoration being transposed onto the screen of the whole world, the whole of cosmic history. The Bible invites us to see the present period of history, from Easter right through to Jesus's second coming to put everything right at last, as held together by and gaining its meaning from these two events. The new creation *has already happened*; that is the good news about the past. The new creation *will happen completely*; that is the good news about the future. That is the larger hope, within which all Christian thinking about the future ought to be framed.

In other words, our hope is not simply that we will go to heaven and there rejoin our loved ones, and of course be with Jesus. All this we are promised; but if we grab at this and forget the larger picture, we will be like a child who is so engrossed with the first sand castle on the beach that he never even notices the glorious and inviting sea. Our personal hopes for what happens after death are fully taken into account within the much, much larger reality we are promised: the new heaven and the new earth, in which God's justice and joy and peace and love will grow like flowers

on every roadside and come like showers on every spring morning. When we long for that new creation, we get our personal
hopes thrown in. When we reverse the focus, putting our personal hopes at the center, we introduce a distortion into the entire
gospel that, like the other distortions we have noted, can produce
long-term damaging results. The good news, in other words, is
not all about me. It is all about God and God's creation—God's
new creation, which results from the covenant renewal that has
been effected through the coronation of Jesus as Israel's Messiah
and the world's rightful lord.

6

Wrong Future,
Wrong Present

L ike the good news about what *has* happened in the past, the good news about what *will* happen in the future has proved hard to grasp. There is a powerful reason for this, which I will come to in a moment. For now, let's just note some of the other lesser ones.

To begin with, there is a popular myth about the early Christians that has been widely put about in the last century or so. According to this myth, the first Christians expected the end of the world almost immediately. When it didn't come, they panicked and changed course, altering some basic elements of the early message. Of course, this makes it seem as though Jesus and Paul were wrong about the future, which presumably means (though many people have tried to deny this) that they may have also been wrong about lots of other things. But that's not the point at the

(so what?)

people still think this

moment. My point here is that this account of early Christian hope is a myth.

A myth isn't just an untruth. It's a story people tell to provide a framework for other things they believe, for other aspects of their life. This modern myth about an early Christian end-of-the-world expectation provided just that: a framework for some things that highly influential interpreters wanted to say.

Some wanted to say that the early Christians had a valid and important religious experience but that they expressed this in the language and imagery of the day—which means end-of-the-world language. According to these interpreters, they really did believe the world would shortly end, but since we know they were mistaken we can strip away this language and get back to the pure experience underneath. Attempts to do this have been notably unsuccessful.

Others have wanted to see the early Christians as having an experience similar to many European thinkers in the twentieth century. The early twentieth century saw many movements, notably the rise of Russian communism and of the Nazi Party in Germany, which claimed to be the natural and inevitable results of historical forces. (All this goes back to thinkers like Marx, and particularly Hegel, in the nineteenth century.) Many thinkers, both Christian and atheist, were hoping that something new would happen to break into this dangerous sequence: a new messianic moment. They were disappointed. Nothing happened, except a disastrous war with millions dead and Europe left with gaping wounds and a legacy of horror. It was in this period that the idea took hold that the early Christians suffered a major disappointment when "the End" failed to arrive on schedule. This was, in fact, a back projection of a modern phenomenon.

A much wiser starting point is to consider the Jewish world of the first century. The Jews of Jesus's day were living on hope. Israel's God had made lavish and grandiose promises, and many

Jews believed it was time for these to be fulfilled. But the promises in question were not only about the Jews of the day being rescued from political enemies and social evils, or about the glorious return of their God to live in person in the Temple once more. These promises were always linked to a larger hope for creation, the hope we noted in the previous chapter in connection with passages like Isaiah 11 or Psalm 96. So writers who wanted to paint a picture of the glorious future often used language that, to an untrained eye many centuries later, might look as though it was predicting the end of the world.

But in fact, in a tradition many hundreds of years old, language like that was never meant to be taken literally. When Isaiah spoke (in chap. 13) of the sun being turned into darkness and the moon into blood, his readers knew that he was talking about the catastrophic fall of great world powers, in this case Babylon. When Jeremiah used end-of-the-world language to describe the fall of Jerusalem long before it happened, he lived for many years in the fear that Jerusalem wouldn't fall and he would therefore turn out to be a false prophet. But he never worried about being thought a false prophet because the world had not come to an end. Thus, though it is quite possible that some people *did* think the space-time universe would end, there is no reason to suppose that this was the natural and intended meaning of that kind of imagery, or that the writers of the New Testament, borrowing that ancient Jewish imagery, envisaged cosmic collapse. *vs earth.*

Here again readers of the New Testament have made the mistake of forgetting (often because of the split-level universe they live in) that language about such things as sun, moon, and stars falling from heaven was about what we would call *political* events. This opens the possibility of finding a new way through an old puzzle. Jesus spoke of certain things that were to happen "within a generation." Many modern readers have supposed that he was talking about "the end of the world," and that he was wrong. But,

language. like numbers

in those famous passages in the Gospels, Jesus is talking not about the end of the world but about *the fall of Jerusalem*. The central passage here, makes this abundantly clear. And of course Jerusalem did indeed fall to the Romans about forty years after the end of Jesus's public career.

What language could a devout Jew, familiar with the scriptures and the great traditions, use to describe such an event, so appalling in itself and in its meaning? We who are familiar with horrors like the terrible events of September 11, 2001, must first imagine a people far more localized than the inhabitants of a modern city, then think of a small ancient city crowded not only with people but with promises—biblical promises of God's blessing and protection. Next imagine, not two great towers crashing to the earth but the whole city, including its enormous and impressive Temple, being burned to the ground. If we had witnessed and survived the destruction of New York or London, what language would do justice to such an event? We would quickly find ourselves running out of ordinary words. We would reach for the language of cosmic catastrophe: the end of the world. That is what the first-century Jews did. Not because it *was* the end of the space-time universe but because it was the end of *their* world. That is how the language worked.

This also explains something else. Jesus continually warned his fellow countrymen that if they didn't follow where he was leading, the result would be disaster. He used quite lurid language for these warnings. Even so, the message didn't really get through. He wasn't saying what they wanted him to say. But a lot of those warnings, taken out of context and interpreted through the lens of much later medieval beliefs, made it sound as though Jesus was warning people not that their city and nation would be destroyed but that they were going to hell. "Unless you repent," he says twice in the early paragraphs of Luke 13, "you will all be destroyed in the same way." Read that in the fifteenth century, and it's obvious what it means: unless you give up your sins, you will be thrown into hell for all eternity. Read it in the first century, and a very different meaning should be equally obvious: unless you turn from your crazy path of nationalist rebellion against Rome, Rome will come and do to you what it has done to everyone who stands in its path. Jesus's contemporaries took no notice. The warnings came true.

This doesn't, by itself, mean that there isn't a prediction of final punishment in the New Testament. There is. But a majority of the sayings that are regularly seen that way do not mean what people have assumed they mean.

Now that we've got that out of the way, more important questions appear. There is one large problem in particular that makes any Christian vision of the future difficult. Once again we find the legacy of the Enlightenment. This time, we need to examine the doctrine of progress.

The Problem with Progress

Doctrine—isn't that a strong, almost Christian word for a philosophical teaching? Yes, and that is exactly how *progress* is used. I spoke two chapters ago about the way the scientific discoveries and political innovations of the eighteenth century gave rise to the view that this caused human history to turn a vital corner, so that everything must now be seen in a new light. "Now that we live in the modern age . . . ," people say, meaning, "Don't you know that we left superstition and ignorance behind? Can't you catch up?"

This viewpoint has generated a powerful belief that *history is automatically going somewhere,* with that somewhere being a steadily more free, open, liberal, or tolerant society. This, people believe, is now inevitable. We can't stand in its way, and we shouldn't try to do so. In other words, the secular world of the last two centuries has got its own vision of the future and the way that future will arrive. And this is radically at odds with the Christian vision of God's remaking of heaven and earth. As with the chronological snobbery of the eighteenth century, which we discussed in chapter 4, so now with what we might call the eschatological snobbery of progress. The world is going where it needs to go; all we have to do is to get on board and we'll get there.

Part of the energy behind this secular ideal of progress comes from the split-level universe I mentioned. As long as you believe in a God who is somehow involved in the life of the world, even if it's not clear how that works out, there is a sense of a strange guiding hand that steers things this way and that. But when God is packed off upstairs and no longer has an executive office on the ground floor, the people downstairs—and this was always the point—are left to run things their own way. This view was eagerly embraced, for cultural, social, and political reasons, in the eighteenth century, long before the scientific discoveries of the nineteenth century (I am thinking of Darwin in particular), which led to the powerful hypothesis that animal species evolved from one another over long periods of time. But when these discoveries came to light, they were eagerly seized on, not simply to show that creation didn't happen in one six-day period roughly six thousand years ago, but to demonstrate that the physical universe had its own ways of running itself *without divine intervention or interference*. God lived upstairs; Darwin's discoveries were taken as proof not only that the staircase had been blocked off but that it had been demolished altogether.

This conclusion did not follow from the discovery of evidence for biological evolution. It was the result of claiming something no scientific discovery could ever actually prove, namely that the universe was indeed split. People had believed that, for quite other reasons, for many years. But in the popular mind this sequence has been forgotten. It is generally assumed that progress is built into the way the world is. And that science proves it.

The thinking went like this. If the downstairs world—the things we can see and measure and study—was, so to speak, doing its own thing, it was a short step to the further conclusion that this downstairs world was moving in one direction. Again, this represented a huge leap from scientific theory to metaphysical speculation, but there were plenty of influential people who wanted the metaphysics and so were eager to co-opt the science. Darwin proposed—and again this was in line with earlier eighteenth-century ideas—that species did not evolve at random. They evolved *because they were better fitted to survive.* Thus the downstairs world was not simply developing in various directions, some of which might be better (by what standard?) and some worse. The universe had an inbuilt tendency to *progress.*

Again, ideas do not catch on just because some scientist makes a discovery. They gain popularity because this is what a lot of people want to believe. Europeans in the nineteenth century, flushed with technological success, developing new empires, conquering the world, really did believe that everything was rapidly getting better. An unquenchable optimism was in the air. The new world was emerging—evolving, you might say—because it was fitter. The old one had better make room for it. It wasn't just that a new era had begun in the eighteenth century. It was that this new moment had unleashed a chain reaction at every level—social, moral, political, and economic. There was, in all things, a kind of built-in life force driving toward improvement. All we had to do was get on board.

One of the truly extraordinary things about recent history is that, despite the events of the twentieth century, people still believe all this. You might have thought that two world wars, the Gulag and Auschwitz, stock market crashes, famines and tribal conflicts in Africa, the desperate plight of the Balkans, and the recent atrocities of violent fundamentalists would make people pause, scratch their heads, and wonder whether progress is still on track. That doesn't seem to happen. People in the Western world still assume that whenever there is a crisis it's important to be on the right side of history. Somehow we are supposed to have privileged access to information (a) that history is moving in a particular direction, (b) that we know what that direction is, and (c) that the direction is toward universal liberal democracy on the Western model. This facile optimism—progress in practice, if you like—has already led to disastrous decision making and may do so again.

In particular, progress is invoked in the two areas where it can be least assumed: the political and the moral. Yes, we can build faster and safer airliners. Yes, we can cure more diseases. Yes, we can even fight crime more successfully. But no, this doesn't mean that our political systems will produce either wisdom or utopia. And no, this doesn't mean that moral principles are automatically moving in a liberal direction—whatever that may be. (An example of the latter, which would be funny if it wasn't so horrendous, occurred in early 2014, when it emerged that some senior figures on the left in British politics had, in their youthful days in the 1970s, supported all kinds of sexual liberation movements, including the pedophile demand to lower the age of consent to four years old.)

The question of progress has been debated at a serious level by leading philosophers and public intellectuals. In the United States, Stephen Pinker argued in his blockbuster *The Better Angels of Our Nature* that the world is demonstrably becoming more peaceful, less violent, less prone to murder and mayhem. In the United Kingdom, John Gray has argued in a string of books for exactly the opposite point of view: progress was always a myth, and even those aspects that had some plausibility have now run out of steam. There may be a sense in which both are true. The global village may have learned some hard lessons and realized that violence usually makes things worse, not better. But a glance around today's world reveals little cause for optimism. Even if Pinker is right about the way things have gone in recent centuries (despite all evidence to the contrary), that doesn't mean things will go on getting more peaceful forever. As soon as a significant number of people run out of food or water, violence will break out again.

All this means that the wider secular world has long given up on the hope expressed in Isaiah 11 or Psalm 96, let alone in Romans 8, 1 Corinthians 15, or Revelation 21 and 22. If there is a glorious future ahead, it will come through progress. Not through anything God does—which is what those passages have in mind.

This leaves open the question of whether progress comes because humans drive it forward or whether it happens all by itself, with humans as the grateful spectators and beneficiaries. (This is actually the secular equivalent of first-century discussions about the kingdom of God: Would God bring it to fruition all by himself, would humans have to do it for him, or would it be some combination of the two?) Did getting rid of divine interference mean also getting rid of human interference? For the people who, as we say, made history in the last two hundred years, the answer was obvious. Progress is coming, but we have to help it on its way.

Of course, it all depends on what you think of as progress. Many people in Western Europe saw the early years of the Soviet Union as the shape of the future. Some thought in the 1930s that Hitler was the answer to Europe's problems. The people who had lived in that world, hoping for a better future to emerge from some secret inner process, then faced the cruel disappointments of the 1940s. That brings us full circle to the social context in which some people guessed at a similar disappointment for the early

Christians. The millennium—the great moment of redemption, the bright future that had glimmered over the horizon—failed to arrive on schedule.

That is the context in which, in the last fifty years in Europe and America, we have seen the rise of a serious antiprogress movement, known loosely as postmodernism. Thinkers like Michel Foucault, Jacques Derrida, and Jean-François Lyotard have done their best to expose the dark roots of the modernist dream of progress. This movement has made a lot of noise, but it hasn't really affected the way public figures think and talk. It hasn't stopped people from acting out the modernist dream that the Western powers are truly progressive, advanced countries who have the obligation and the right to call the rest of the world to fall into line (and to help it on its way with well-meaning intervention). Of course, the rest of the world takes little notice. But since that doesn't fit the model, this just produces incomprehension among Western leaders. Our politicians and opinion makers find themselves asking, "Can't those unenlightened folk see we're right? Shouldn't they be getting on the right side of history?"

Good News—for the World?

These questions about the future have dominated recent Western discussion. Where does that leave the Christian vision?

Once again the church has regularly gone along for the ride. At times of social optimism, it has been easy for the church to talk grandly about the evangelization of the world in this generation. At times of social disaster, some Christians have seen world history simply in terms of things getting darker and darker as a prelude to God doing something radically new, shining a new light into the pitch-black darkness of a post-Christian world. Both are easy reactions, but neither really grasps the good news of the gospel.

Here we have to maintain a balance that history shows to be very difficult. On the one hand, some people will shrug their shoulders and say there's nothing we can do to make the world a better place until Jesus returns. All we can do is alleviate some of the worst evils and look after those who are suffering. This simply ignores the New Testament's emphasis.

The risen Jesus already claims all authority in heaven and on earth. Paul, sometimes writing from prison, speaks in grandiose terms of the Messiah already reigning, of his having defeated all the powers of heaven and earth. The early Christians were not fools. They were not whistling in the dark. They were not claiming that everything was just fine and getting finer by the minute. They faced persecution, prison, suffering, and death on a scale unimaginable to most comfortable Western Christians today. But they didn't give up saying what they said about the *present* reign of Jesus. And they saw their own work as somehow bound up with that. Paul, at the end of his remarkable chapter on the resurrection (1 Cor. 15), declares that because of the coming resurrection, "the work you're doing will not be worthless." Somehow, in ways we cannot at present discern, what is done in the present out of love for God and in the power of the Spirit will be part of God's new world when it finally arrives.

Thus it won't do to say there is nothing that can be done to improve matters before Jesus returns. Yes, the second coming will accomplish all sorts of things of which at present we can only dream. I do not expect to see the wolf lying down with the lamb within the present state of creation, and if I were to meet a lion in the street (fortunately, an unlikely event in eastern Scotland), I would not rely on its having read Isaiah 11 and knowing that it should now be vegetarian. But whenever someone says that there is no point in working for justice in the world; whenever anyone says that it doesn't matter what we do to the planet because God is going to throw it away one day and leave us in heaven instead;

whenever anyone says that there is no point in working for unity in the church, for reconciliation between different nations, cultures, and ethnic groups—then we must protest. *Jesus the Messiah is risen from the dead!* A new world has come into being, and within that new world all kinds of new possibilities are now open.

This was the mood in which the early Christians—despite the Roman Empire's best effort to persecute them and stamp out the movement—began to live lives of generosity, caring for the poor, and tending the sick, including people with whom they had no connection either through family or through work. They realized, as they worshipped the God they saw in Jesus and celebrated his good news, that a new way of being human had been launched. They looked at impossibilities and prayed their way through them. They were mocked and vilified, attacked and driven out of communities. But the work went on. New things happened. People saw the difference. The resurrection of Jesus launched a new, and newly *integrated,* way of life. All that stood in the way of justice and peace—all the selfish concerns, petty jealousies, ambitions and rivalries and sheer human nastiness—belonged to the old world, to the old age that had been superseded by the new world of Easter. The power of evil that had lent its weight to injustice and oppression for so many centuries had been defeated on the cross.

Thus the early Christians prayed and acted on the basis that the good news was true. There is no reason on earth, and certainly none in heaven, why we today should not do the same. And if anyone tries to say that the good news is not about all these things—about freeing slaves, about helping the poor, about reconciling warring factions, ethnic groupings, and whole nations, about looking after the blessed world we live on and in—but instead is only about coming to faith in the present and going to heaven in the future, then we must reply that something has gone very, very wrong in their thinking.

According to the Bible, the death and resurrection of Jesus—the very heart of the good news—are the foundation of God's new world. There is no reason why we should not pray and work for signs of that new world to be born even in the midst of the old age, of the world that is still, as Paul says, "groaning in labor-pains." In fact, there are excellent reasons for making these efforts a major preoccupation. Despite what skeptics and critics sometimes say, followers of Jesus have transformed the world in all sorts of ways in the last two thousand years. It was Jesus's followers, after all, who went about caring for the poor, tending the sick, and providing education for people of all sorts (not only the rich or the elite). There is no reason why Jesus's followers should not continue this work and every reason why they should.

But as with every statement of Christian truth, this can easily be distorted. Some Christians have imagined that the Christian task is to build the kingdom of God by our own efforts here and now. Often this social gospel imperative has gained energy as compassionate believers have looked at the complacent church on the one hand and the plight of the poor on the other, and have realized which side of the street Jesus would be standing on. That is a natural and (to my mind) proper reaction. But as it stands, it won't do. God's kingdom is God's kingdom, not ours. God will bring his final new day as and when he pleases. We are not engaged in building the kingdom by ourselves. Only God builds God's kingdom, and he will do that fully and finally in his own time and his own way.

But—and this point, again, is often missed—we can and must work *for* God's kingdom, to produce advance signs of his saving rule, his holiness, his justice, his joy, his celebration of every good thing. We can do this because we stand on the ground of the resurrection, believing that the forces of darkness have been put in their place and a new light has been born. The Christian church, throughout its history, has always known that God was calling it to this kind of work and witness. Everything we have said in this book about the good news points in the same direction.

We could sum up all of this in five propositions, which need to be held in balance. First, the lordship of the risen Jesus, who has launched his new creation in the middle of the present old one, means that real and lasting change is *possible* at personal, social, cultural, national, and global levels. It has happened (think of the abolition of the slave trade), and it can happen again. Individual lives can be transformed from top to bottom by the power of the good news, as the Spirit applies the death and resurrection of Jesus to the mind, heart, and life. And that can happen with whole communities, too.

Second, though, is a point we too easily forget: real and lasting change is *costly*. The principalities and powers that have run the world in their destructive fashion for so long won't release their deadly grip without a struggle. Yes, the basic victory has been won on the cross. But as the first generations of Jesus followers quickly discovered, this victory is put into practice through the suffering they themselves undergo as they share the messianic path. Jesus warned that this would be so. Paul and other early writers constantly emphasized it. But—and here's the point—they also emphasized that this suffering, whatever form it takes, is the way the true signs of God's kingdom will appear on earth as in heaven.

Third, therefore, real and lasting change in everything from personal to global life is always *sporadic*. It is never smooth, linear progress. Christians sometimes sing hymns about "advancing from glory to glory," as though the victory of the good news were being implemented step by step until, at last, the earth would be full of divine glory as the waters cover the sea. Half an hour reading church history would soon dispel this illusion. The great churches of the first three centuries—in the Middle East, Egypt and North Africa, and Turkey—have vanished almost without trace. There have been great losses as well as great gains. Complacency, whether personal or corporate, is always dangerous. The music of the gospel is not moving in a steady crescendo toward a glorious climax. In particular, there is always a danger that the followers of Jesus, glimpsing some part of his new creation, will seize upon it and make it their agenda to be pursued to the exclusion of all else. Distortions and distractions are always nudging at our elbows.

But fourth, there is an equal and opposite danger that Christians, recognizing the danger of a triumphalist progress of the gospel, will retreat once more into gloom and negativity. True, real and lasting change in the present time will not bring God's kingdom all by itself, but such real and lasting change *genuinely anticipates* God's final kingdom, points toward it, and gives a foretaste of that ultimate reality. When the children of Israel made their first advance toward the promised land, they sent out spies, who brought back a bunch of grapes so the people could see taste the fruit even before they had claimed their inheritance (Num. 13). In the same way, the real and lasting changes brought about by the good news in the lives of individuals and communities are not accidental luxuries. They are real signs and foretastes of what is to come. (Of course, we should remind ourselves that, despite that sign, the Israelites rebelled, refused to believe the promises, and had to wait another generation before at last inheriting the land.)

Fifth, therefore, it is vital that those who believe the good news work tirelessly for real and lasting change in individual lives, the church, and the wider world. When we say, "Jesus is Lord," we are not whistling in the dark. When we say that God's new creation really began with Jesus's resurrection, we are reminding ourselves where we truly are on God's map. When we pray for God's holy Spirit to breathe in and through our lives, it is so that new life— real and lasting new life—may spring up in the world. Yes, there will be setbacks. Yes, there will be suffering. We can never suppose that God's purposes will go forward automatically and all we have to do is to get on board. Often the results of our work will only be apparent some time later—perhaps after our own lifetimes. *But the good news is true.* Something has happened as a result of which the world is a different place. We can be part of it. If we are following Jesus, praying for his Spirit to guide and empower us, we are already part of it. We can be, and we are called to be, good-news people—people who themselves are being renewed by the good news, people through whom the good news is bringing healing and hope to the world at whatever level.

I will have more to say in the last chapter about how, through prayer, we can become good-news people of that sort. But for the moment I want to focus on the deeply personal meaning of the gospel. For many today, of course, the personal is the only meaning they know. I have tried to expand that horizon to its full biblical scope. But it would be strange if, in doing so, we failed to highlight and celebrate the personal transformation that has always been at the heart of the good news.

Good News—for You Personally

If the good news really is what it says, there is all the room in the world for delighted celebration of the gospel in the life of every child, woman, and man. To miss this element—to think of Christianity without this deeply personal aspect—is like turning up at your own birthday party to find everyone having a great time but nobody getting around to wishing you a happy birthday. The good news, as applied to every single person, is indeed a birthday party—a birthday party for the new creation, *to which you and I are invited so it can be our birthday party, too.* This is what people often mean by preaching the gospel: to announce Jesus and his death and resurrection in such a way that people, believing it, come to what some biblical writers call new birth. *The rescue and transformation that God effected in the death and resurrection of Jesus is to become the rescue and transformation of every person.* That is the challenge of faith, because the gospel message, working powerfully through God's Spirit in the hearts and minds of human beings, produces that faith: the confession that Jesus is Lord and the heartfelt belief that God really did raise him from the dead. That faith is the first sign of new life, and Paul declares that God will complete in the end the work he has begun in us.

Christian spirituality—an awareness of the loving and guiding presence of God, sorrow for sin and gratitude for forgiveness, the possibility and challenge of prayer, a love for God and for our neighbors, the desire for holiness and the hard moral work it requires, the gradual or sudden emergence of particular vocations, a lively hope for God's eventual new creation—is generated by the good news of what *has* happened in the past and what *will* happen in the future. All this and much, much more is what is meant by the good news in the present.

But this, again, doesn't mean that we already have in the present everything that God wants to give us. Far from it. Any Christian with self-knowledge knows that there is a long, long way to go. None of us as individuals and none of our work done for the kingdom will get us to the point where we are complete as Christians, or complete as a church, ready for Jesus to reappear as merely an added bonus. No. That moment, when it comes, will be a radical new awakening, and all kinds of things about the present world, including death itself, will then disappear for the first time. Just as Jesus, Israel's Messiah, did not appear with a flourish of trumpets as the nation prepared for his coming but rather to the surprise of an unready nation, so we may suppose it will be when God eventually renews the world.

One famous passage where this point is strikingly made is the third chapter of Paul's letter to the Philippians. There he gives his readers an example to imitate: he, Paul, has suffered the loss of his previous status and prestige so that he may have the Messiah as his profit. This, he says, "means knowing him, knowing the power of his resurrection, and knowing the partnership of his sufferings. It means sharing the form and pattern of his death, so that somehow I may arrive at the final resurrection from the dead" (3:10–11). That gets the balance exactly right: the Messiah's presence, life, and power already belong to us, though always marked by the cross. And—just in case anyone has missed the point—Paul continues, "I'm not implying that I've already received 'resurrection,' or that I've already become complete and mature!" (3:12). He is still on the way. "Those of us who are mature," he says with deliberate irony, "should think like this" (3:15); in other words, the sure sign of Christian maturity is that you know you haven't arrived yet. Challenges remain; it's easy to become complacent and sink back into the old ways (3:18–19). But the real transformation, which is already true, is the signpost to the ultimate transformation, which is yet to come when Jesus returns to heal and restore the whole creation, and ourselves as part of it (3:20–21). As with all good news, we live in the present between the event that *has happened* and the event that *is yet to happen*. The real and lasting change the gospel produces in individual human lives is shaped at every point by that past event and that future event. That is why, though there is never reason for complacency, there is always good reason for joy, as Paul stresses in the passage that follows (4:1, 4).

Getting the Balance Right

The good news, then, is good news about the present as well as the past and the future. Despite the secular claim that all real advances in the world are the result of secular modernism, and despite the barrage of hostility launched against the church by some new atheists, it remains the case that the church has, for two millennia, been in the forefront of education, medicine, and care of the poor. Real and lasting change has happened. Lives have been transformed.

One striking result is that the Christian good news has generated some of the finest works of art and music known to the human race. These cannot be gainsaid. One such work, which illustrates the difficulty the church has had in keeping a balance in thinking about the future, is the wonderful oratorio *Messiah* by George Frideric Handel. It consists entirely of settings of biblical texts. The selection and arrangement of those texts, the work of Handel's collaborator Charles Jennens, reflect the excited optimism of the early eighteenth century (the work was first performed in 1742). In those days, many believed that, by the newfound energy for preaching the gospel, all the nations of the world would come to believe in Jesus and the entire globe would be living gladly and fruitfully under the wise rule of the One True God. Thus the middle section of the three-part oratorio focuses on the death and resurrection of Jesus, and then on the preaching of the gospel throughout the world, the pacification of the warring nations by the Messiah's worldwide rule, and finally the great shout of Hallelujah—perhaps the most famous thing Handel ever wrote—because "the kingdom of this world is become the kingdom of our Lord and of his Christ." (That is the translation of Rev. 11:15 used in the oratorio; a more literal one might be "the kingdom of the world has passed to our Lord and his Messiah.") This coming of the kingdom, we note, happens at the end of the global preaching of the gospel, *not* at the time of the resurrection of the dead and the new creation. That comes later. First is the worldwide rule of Jesus, brought about through the normal processes of preaching the gospel. Then, after a glorious period, the final events, including the new heaven and earth and the general resurrection.

But this sense of Christian hope dwindled with the eighteenth century for many reasons. Instead, many missionaries saw their task not as claiming the world for its rightful lord but as snatching a few souls from the fire. As though in reaction to the secular optimism of the day, and in line with the split-level world in which people were no longer looking for the kingdom to come on earth as in heaven but rather simply to go to heaven, the work of the gospel was conceived in terms of a rescue operation. The kingdom was not of this world. The hope was simply for heaven. Earth could be left to its own devices, along with its unrepentant inhabitants.

Thus the mood swings of European and American Christianity, which have been so influential in much of the rest of the world, came and went between the eighteenth and twentieth centuries, producing the wide range of approaches in evidence today. On the one hand, we have fundamentalist dispensationalists awaiting a rapture in which Jesus will return to snatch them up to heaven. On the other hand, we have the liberal mainstream churches, especially in America, who, perhaps in reaction, often seem to have given up talk of any future, personal or corporate, other than that which can be achieved through social policies in the present age. This is not a healthy state of affairs. And it all stems from the failure to grasp how the gospel works as good news.

How can we draw all this together? The good news about what *happened* in the events concerning Jesus was foolishness and scandal in Jesus's time and remains so to this day. It now appears that the good news about what *will happen* in the new creation is also foolishness and scandal in the modern Western world and, alas, in many parts of the modern Western church. But recognizing this pattern ought to give us hope. When Saint Paul spoke of his gospel as being about Jesus the Messiah, "a scandal to Jews and folly to Gentiles," he went on to say that it was also "to those who are called, Jews and Greeks alike, the Messiah—God's power and God's wisdom" (1 Cor. 1:23–24). The church needs to recover its nerve and talk about the good news once more *as* good news, not good advice—as good news that will appear bizarre to some and shocking to others but will carry, as before, the salvation and wise power and love of the one God.

All this points to the question implicit in much of this book. The gospel, Paul said, is about the unveiling of *God's* power, of *God's* wisdom. He rubs in the point: "God's folly is wiser than humans, you see, and God's weakness is stronger than humans" (1 Cor. 1:25). This is an odd thing to say. It certainly isn't the way people in today's culture think about God. But that's the point. At the heart of the strange, challenging, and shocking good news, there lies the ultimate good news: good news about God himself.

It would be possible after setting out the shape of the good news (past event and future hope) to explore in more detail what this good news means for life in between. How does holding fast to the idea of good news rather than good advice affect the Christian life? There is much that could be said on that topic. In particular, it would be good to explore how, in today's world as in the first century, the political challenge of the gospel might be given full rein. Good news was, as we have seen, a slogan used by the early Roman emperors to announce their ascension to the throne or some great military victory or other celebration. Granted that Paul was drawing on the ancient Israelite belief in the good news of Israel's God overthrowing the forces of paganism and liberating his people, how did this essentially Jewish message confront the paganism and the empires of his own day? And how might that translate into our very different world today? Those are important questions, and it would take another whole book to deal with them properly.

We could also appropriately discuss how the human vocation
to share in God's rule over the world is then translated (as in the
book of Acts) into the human vocation to share in the rule of Jesus
the Messiah over the world—a vocation effected, as Jesus's rule,
through suffering, misunderstanding, persecution, and in some
cases violent death. And it would be possible to show, as we did in
the case of the past good news and the future good news, various
cultural and philosophical reasons why it has been difficult for the
world as a whole, and indeed for the church within that world,
to maintain the right balance in all this. In particular, it would
be possible to show how, in the life of every believer, constantly
looking back to the original good news prevents any sense of
merely human achievement, and constantly looking forward to
the future good news prevents any sense of merely human ambi-
tion. When the good news collapses into good advice, we can pat
ourselves on the back for taking that advice and doing our bit.
When it remains good news, we take no credit. We have simply
found ourselves confronted, challenged, and transformed by this
good news, and we live out of the gratitude that is the proper response to undeserved grace.

All this, as I say, we could deal with in considerably more detail. But it is time to move to the real depths of the good news:
God himself. All that we have said so far about Jesus points to
this. What happens when we ask the question? What happens
when we mention God in polite society?

7

Surprised by God

THE WORD *God* is a heavy, clunky little syllable. It drops like a lead weight into otherwise cheerful conversations. It sticks in the throat like a lump of undercooked dumpling. It comes up over the horizon like a sudden cloud, blotting out the sun. The very sound of the word in English (and in German, where the hard *Gott* has the same effect) reflects the way most people in modern Western culture now think.

All this is, of course, a mere linguistic accident. But I think for many people it reflects something of the bad press God has had in our culture. The Greek word *theos* feels somehow gentler, more poetic; the Hebrew *Elohim*, more mysterious. The blunt monosyllable *God* all too easily gives a double wrong impression: first, that God is an object in our world that can be discussed as such; second, that such a being is a monolithic little dictator who sits there giving orders. Actually, in and of itself the word doesn't suggest that, of course, but its blunt, clunky sound easily goes with the popular image of God as a bully in the sky who makes odd demands and becomes dangerously petulant if people ignore him. For many people, the idea that there is a God would be *bad* news, not good news.

Most people today, in short, assume that the word *God* refers to a dull, distant, and perhaps dangerous being. Most of those who think like that try hard, not surprisingly, to believe that this being doesn't exist. "I don't believe in God," said the novelist Kingsley Amis, "and I hate him."

They are right.

That God—the dull, distant, and dangerous one—does not exist.

This book has been about the one that does.

The first Christians lived in a world of many gods. There were the big, well-known ones. In Greece, they were called Zeus, Poseidon, Artemis, and so on; in the Roman world, their names were Jupiter, Neptune, Diana, and the rest. There were gods of the sea and the city; gods of the hearth and the bridal chamber; gods of war and money, of art and music, gods of just about everything you could think of. And particular gods or goddesses for each place you went. You couldn't go far or get much done without coming across more of them.

Some of the great philosophers scratched their heads, thought about this cheerful divine muddle, and said that really all these gods were different aspects of one true God, who was a secret but powerful presence in every part of the world. Others, faced with the same evidence, said that the gods might exist but if they did they were far away, they weren't interested in us, and they certainly didn't intervene in our world.

Most people, however, continued to believe in the dangerous presence of the confused divine jumble. In particular, the popular belief then, as now, was that these gods were out to get you—perhaps because you'd done things they didn't like or simply because they didn't like you in the first place. When these philosophers came up with theories, they weren't just trying to make sense of the strange world we live in. They were trying to get rid of the idea of the big bully in the sky. If there is no god, you can relax and enjoy your life. Perhaps.

The extraordinary thing is that over and over again, in Western culture at least, people have faced similar questions and come up with similar answers—each time supposing that they had made a new discovery. The ancient philosophers, as we just saw, didn't like the old bullies in the sky, so they found ways of saying either that the divine was a force within all things or that any gods which might or might not exist were completely detached from us. The first lot scrunch together the gods and the world; the second send the gods packing upstairs—perhaps out of the house altogether—and let the world run itself however it wants. In the Middle Ages, the old bully in the sky made a comeback in the church, threatening people with hell, or at least purgatory, and demanding to have his hideous wrath appeased.

There were two reactions. Philosophers from the Renaissance to the present day split God apart from the world. As we have seen, the Western Enlightenment went that route, pushing God upstairs out of sight and allowing natural processes to do whatever they want down here on terra firma. But the Reformers, and then the Puritans, and then many other Christian movements such as the early Methodists, had a different reaction. They stressed the saving death of Jesus as the means by which the wrath of God had been averted. Often this was accompanied by great gratitude and love. Often, however, it has left the semipagan vision of God untouched. That then produced a further reaction, which is where the modern angry atheists come in.

That movement suddenly became very visible a few years ago in the United Kingdom. Some militant atheists decided to announce a kind of upside-down good news. They paid for large advertisements on London buses, which read, "There's probably no God: now stop worrying and enjoy your life." (There had been some debate about the word *probably,* but they stuck with it. If they had said, "There is no God," they might have been prosecuted for advertising something they couldn't prove—a very British compromise.) I heard that the campaign even attracted funding from one or two Christian organizations because it helped to put the question of God on the public agenda. An interesting, if risky, move.

The campaign was fascinating for many reasons, but particularly because of what it took for granted. It assumed that if there was a God, this would mean we would all spend our time worrying, whereas if there wasn't one, we could all relax. It was assumed that any God which might exist would be keen to stop us from enjoying ourselves. (I once knew a man who complained to me, "Everything Jesus is against, I like.") In particular, it was taken for granted that the God Christians talk about is that sort of God—the killjoy type. The message on the buses thus announced good news—the good news that the atheists had discovered this God didn't exist after all. We could all heave a sigh of relief.

This line of thought ("Help! There's a God who's out to get us! No, there isn't—no such being exists!") is not a modern discovery. It goes back at least to the fifth century BC, when some philosophers began to suggest that the world runs itself without divine intervention. But what I have been concerned about in this book is clarifying what the first followers of Jesus meant when *they* talked about good news, in order to clarify what that might mean for us today.

Part of our problem is that Western culture still has a legacy of Deism. Deism, a largely seventeenth- and eighteenth-century phenomenon, is basically halfway to that split-level world. This philosophy imagined God as an absentee landlord; he might have made the world in the first place (thus rescuing part of the Jewish and Christian view), but he had now left it to its own devices (thus collapsing into a practical atheism). At the same time, however, because he had made the world in the first place, he still got the blame for everything that went wrong on his property.

That is where many people still are today. They aren't sure whether they believe in God or not, but they are quite prepared to tell him off for making a mess of things. As one of Woody Allen's characters put it, "If it turns out that there *is* a God, I don't think that he's evil. I think that the worst you can say about him is that basically he's an underachiever." Another e-mail came in while I was redrafting this chapter. "If God is in charge, and God is loving," asked my correspondent, "how could he have screwed things up so badly?"

This Deism—"God the Father not quite almighty, living a long way away in heaven, maker but not sustainer of earth"—is still the default mode for most of Western culture. That is why people have found it difficult to join the dots between this God and Jesus. What might it mean to start with this idea of God and try to fit Jesus into it? Not much. It doesn't make sense—which is why many, including many who still call themselves Christians, are puzzled by the whole idea of the divinity of Jesus. For the early Christians, though, it was quite different. They saw it the other way around. They believed that it was only when you looked hard at Jesus that you understood what the true God was like.

A Different Kind of God

That's why the stories about Jesus—the four Gospels or good-news books—are quite complicated. They show Jesus not parachuting down from a great height to dispense solutions to all problems nor zapping everything into shape like some kind of Superman, but living in the mess and muddle of a very difficult part of the world at an especially difficult moment in its history and absorbing the pain and the shame of it all within his own life, within his own body. The Gospels are challenging. They don't wear their theology on their sleeves. They ask us to come into the world of the story and find out what it's like to live there. Answer: Not very comfortable. But massively transforming if you let the story wash over you.

So let's come back to the first century. The first followers of Jesus (Paul and many others) went out into the wider world with what they insisted was good news: There *is* a God, but he's not like the gods you know already. He is like—well, he's like Jesus.

What on earth could have made them want to say that? Part of the answer, of course, is Jesus himself. But it goes beyond that.

The first followers of Jesus were Jews, and the Jews had inherited a millennia-long tradition of beliefs about their very different God. Some of the finest poems ever written grew out of this tradition, and when we start to understand it we can see why. This God was at once far greater and more majestic than any of the other gods and far more intimately and personally involved with the world and with people. He was, on the one hand, the creator of the world, standing outside it and looking at it as a human being might look upon a small heap of ants. On the other hand, he acted in the world with a remarkable blend of power and gentleness. The same prophetic passage which declares that this God "sits above the circle of the earth" and "stretches out the heavens like a curtain" also insists that he "feeds his flock like a shepherd, gathers the lambs in his arms, and gently leads the mother sheep."

It isn't easy to hold this double-sided picture of God in your mind. The ancient Israelites found it difficult, too. But that's the point. To think that the real purpose of our inquiries is to enable us to hold a satisfactory picture of God in our minds is to make a fundamental mistake. Karl Marx said that the point was not to understand the world but to change it. With God—at least, with this strange God of whom the ancient scriptures spoke—the first and most important point was not to understand him but to trust him. The idea that you might begin by looking this God up and down, giving him a cool appraisal, and then, if you understood him and approved of him, you might respond to him, is to deny that he is God at all. If he is God, our primary role is not to analyze him but to worship him; it is not for *us* to figure *him* out but to let *him* figure *us* out. Yes, I know: this sounds like a leap into the unknown. But the alternative is a sure route to idolatry, making a god in your own image.

For centuries the ancient Israelites, often despite themselves, were the guardians of this extraordinary good news. There *was* a God, but he was both far greater and far more intimately involved than the gods of the world around them. The trouble was, the world around seemed to be having it all its own way. It looked as though Israel's God, whom they believed to be the creator of the world, had gone to sleep on the job. Some of the Psalms, the great prayer-poems of ancient Israel, accuse God of doing just that and shout at him to wake up. It looked as though he had forgotten what he was supposed to be doing. The ancient scriptures insisted that there was good news. But for many generations, those who read these scriptures had to swallow hard and go on trying to believe in the face of much evidence to the contrary. They sang songs about this God coming back in power and love to make everything better, put the whole world right, and establish justice and peace in the world. Israel's ancient scriptures used all kinds of vivid pictures to describe what it would be like when that great day came.

Many people in Jesus's day knew these scriptures every bit as well as a music fan today knows the words to the songs in the charts. Except that *these* songs (the Psalms and all those poetic oracles in the prophets) had been around for centuries, and they had been read and chanted—and puzzled over!—for all that time. They were simply part of life, widely known, deeply loved, a source of prayer and hope.

Out of these oracles and songs there emerged several closely related themes. Jesus's contemporaries believed that one day their God would claim his rightful sovereignty over the world. He would rescue his people from their enemies, reestablish them in their land, and come back to live in their midst. And he would fill the whole world with justice and peace. This would naturally mean eliminating wickedness from the world. A vision to inspire hope.

Some writers, both in the Bible and in later Jewish works, seem to have been particularly keen on the last element: that the wicked would be condemned at last. But the main thing was their belief in a God who was radically different from all the gods around them—and their belief that one day he would at last do what he had promised.

They looked around and, apart from occasional signs of hope and life, they saw the non-Jewish world laughing at them. Calling them atheists—oh, the irony of it. But they went on talking about good news, even though they had little idea of when it would arrive and less still about what it would look like when it did.

But then a young man walked into a meeting house in a hill town called Nazareth and announced that the time had come. The good news had arrived. In person.

That, of course, is where we found ourselves in chapter 3. How do we move on from there? What must we say about the God who, however surprisingly, we see in Jesus?

For a start, we must get rid of the popular view of God. It is extraordinary how powerful this image is and how resistant to challenge. No serious thinker has entertained this popular view, but it lingers on. Newspaper cartoons are a good way of assessing the popular conception. Cartoons involving God usually picture him as an old man with a beard, sitting on a cloud a long way above the earth. When Nelson Mandela died in December 2013, there was massive media coverage of the man and his funeral. But there was also a widely reported sideshow. Three world leaders—the president of the United States and the prime ministers of Great Britain and Denmark—took a selfie, a photograph of themselves. Some people thought it was disrespectful. Personally, I think Mandela would have been delighted. He would have wanted to be in the picture himself. But the next day a cartoon appeared in a newspaper. It showed Mandela standing on a cloud beside a white-robed, bearded figure who was taking a selfie of the two of them together. Even God—the God of popular imagination— wanted to get in on the Mandela celebration. And the cartoon didn't have to have to label this white-robed, bearded figure with the word *God*. It was obvious who the artist had in mind.

But is that popular picture correct? Is that old bearded figure, waiting on a cloud to receive the recently dead, even remotely like the God of the Bible, the God whom Paul announced as good news? No.

What then can we say about the God who has been behind our story all along?

All that we have said so far points to three things, each of which counts as good news. Each is also liable to be dismissed by some as scandalous and by others as foolish.

Creator, Judge, Lover

The first is that the one true God is the *creator* of the world. We have thought about this before, but I want to stress here that this really is good news. We are not cast adrift in an alien environment. There's an old hymn that begins, "This is my Father's world." The strange beauty and power we sense in sunlight and starlight, in the majesty of a mountain or the tiny perfection of the smallest flower or insect—all this is the work of the Creator. The glorious sweep of his vast universe and the infinite attention to detail speak of one who has taken, and continues to take, delight in all that he has made.

As I write these lines, the sun is going down, leaving a trail of delicate gray-pink clouds floating on the evening breeze. The light is soft and gentle, making every tree, every building look quietly mysterious. One psalm speaks of God making the entrance and exit of the day to praise him, and I think it was light like this that the poet had in mind. Of course, the rationalist would have no difficulty explaining all this away, but the rest of us can quietly ignore such a shallow attitude and get on with enjoying the view.

This is, of course, all assertion, not proof. I do not claim that I can look at a sunset and deduce a creator. But, as with everything else, that's not how it works. God is not an object in our universe. *We* are objects in *his* universe—and if that's true, it makes sense of the layer upon layer of wonder, delight, beauty, and joy that comes to us through the natural world.

But how might we know it was true? The best answer must be, because of Jesus. Because, in Jesus, we see the same hand at work—and it is also at work addressing the principal problem in any account of God as creator.

The problem is well known, and we've met it already. It's not simply that, as in the Woody Allen quote, God seems to be a bit of an underachiever (as though he were the CEO of a company that's not doing as well as its shareholders expected). It is that in this world of beauty and power, of sunsets and starlight, there are multiple layers of violence, bloodshed, and apparently wanton destruction. There are small creatures, rather a lot of them, who live as parasites inside other larger creatures and whose sole raison d'être appears to be to eat them alive from within. I won't go on; the problem, as I say, is well known.

In fact, the problem can also work the other way. Theologians have written about the problem of evil, but atheists less regularly write about the problem of good. If everything, including my brain and emotions, is the result of random collisions of atoms, why do we find ourselves in such awe and delight at so many things in the world? Can it really all be explained as a legacy of our evolutionary biology? That seems to take reductionism to ridiculous lengths.

However, as I say, it is Jesus who anchors all this. Jesus doesn't give an explanation for the pain and sorrow of the world. He comes where the pain is most acute and takes it upon himself. Jesus doesn't explain why there is suffering, illness, and death in the world. He brings healing and hope. He doesn't allow the problem of evil to be the subject of a seminar. He allows evil to do its worst to him. He exhausts it, drains its power, and emerges with new life. The resurrection says, more clearly than anything else can, "There is a God, and he is the creator of the world we know, and he is the father of Jesus, Israel's Messiah." That is the first part of the good news about God.

The second part, as any reader of this book will by now expect, comes at the other end of the story. The good news about what *has* happened looks ahead to the good news about what *will* happen. The same God who made the world in the first place will restore and renew it in the end.

"The wolf shall live with the lamb, the leopard shall lie down with the kid, the calf and the lion and the fatling together, and a little child shall lead them" (Isa. 11:6). What does this all mean? Why will it happen?

Because "the earth will be full of the knowledge of the LORD [Israel's God, the one they called YHWH] as the waters cover the sea" (Isa. 11:9). Or, in Paul's words, when even death itself has been overcome, God will be "all in all" (1 Cor. 15:28). This is the ultimate good news. Nothing will be lost. All that is good and beautiful, and especially all that has been done out of love for God, out of the power of Jesus's death and new life, and by the leading of the Spirit, will somehow be part of God's new world.

This is the point at which we glimpse how this vision of God brings together the truths hidden in some of the most important old philosophies. The split-level universe, which is the default position for most Westerners today, at least has going for it that the world as it is and God as he is do seem to be out of joint. All is not well; all is not right. *But it will be,* and Jesus's resurrection is the confirmation of that promise, the beginning of its fulfillment, which is then continued in the work of the holy Spirit. At the same time, the philosophies that try to put God, or the gods, and the world into the same bracket, so that the world is full of divinity and divinity is simply the inner life of the world, are trying to get the future promise without the intermediate story of rescue or renewal. God *will* be all in all, but that is not where we are at the moment. That will be the radical application to the whole cosmos of the truth we see in Jesus's resurrection, which depends on the defeat of sin and death that has taken place through Jesus's death. Thus the good news about God is anchored supremely in Jesus.

Between the good news of creation and the good news of the final restoration of all things—the good news of God as creator and God as judge—we find, third and finally, that the God who made the world is the God of infinite, exuberant, lavish, generous *love.* This is the center of the good news.

Think about it this way. God made a world that is other than himself; this, already, is a striking idea that has puzzled great thinkers down the years. If God is perfectly good, why would he make something that, by definition, is less than perfectly good? That question has more of the quirky philosopher about it than the devout worshipper, but let it stand for the moment. The answer must be that God creates not out of need but out of love—out of the generous love that takes delight in his creatures, and especially his human, image-bearing creatures, to whom he has given such responsibility in his world.

It is not God's ultimate intention that the world he has made be always and forever other than himself. He intends that he will be "all in all": that the earth will be full of his knowledge and glory as the waters cover the sea. But the route to that goal—this, of course, is seen with the hindsight of the gospel story—is through the outpouring of his love in Jesus and in the Spirit. *The good news of what happened in Jesus is the central moment in the revelation of the good news that the one true God is the God of utter, self-giving love.*

I have not tried in this book to approach the mysterious depths of meaning hidden in the shameful and cruel death of Jesus. But again and again, the early Christians came back not to theory but to gratitude and to answering love. "This is how we know love: he laid down his life for us" (1 John 3:16). "Love consists in this: not that we loved God, but that he loved us and sent his son to be the sacrifice that would atone for our sins" (1 John 4:10). "We love because he first loved us" (1 John 4:19). "The son of God . . . loved me and gave himself for me" (Gal. 2:20). "This is how God demonstrates his own love for us: the Messiah died for us while we were still sinners" (Rom. 5:8). "He had always loved his own people in the world; now he loved them right through to the end" (John 13:1). This is at the heart of the good news of God. What God *has* done in Jesus and what he *will do* at the end are united and held together in this: that he is the God of utter, generous love.

The thing about love is that it is *creative*. The great medieval Italian poet Dante ended his masterpiece by invoking "the love that moves the sun and the other stars." If today we hear that as a sentimental metaphor, it is because our vision of love is too small. Dante had grasped something deep within the thought of ancient

Israel, deep within the good news of the first followers of Jesus, deep within the mind and heart and vocation of Jesus: the good news that there is indeed a God, a God who made the world, a God who made the world not because he was forced to but because his inmost nature is generous, exuberant love.

This is the basis of all other good news: that the power behind the cosmos is not blind chance, nor yet brute force, but love. It is a delighted love that celebrates the goodness and specialness of every part of creation and of the extraordinary, brilliant, pulsating entirety of it. A love that cares for and cares about the smallest creature and the farthest star. A love that made one creature in particular, humans, to share uniquely in the capacity to receive and to give love, and so to share uniquely in the vocation to work with the grain of the Creator's intention, to bring his work to its wonderful intended fulfillment. There are many things in the world as it now is that conspire to make us forget this great truth. The good news of Jesus is there not only to remind us of it but to transform us with it so that we in turn may become transformative people.

So what does this love do when faced with broken limbs and broken lives? What does it do when confronted by denial and rejection? What does it do when humans who have the capacity to share in the innermost being of the Creator twist that capacity into its opposite, the capacity to hate and sneer and spit and snarl, to kick and stab and wound and kill? Does love then say, "Well, perhaps love is all very well when things are going fine, but now that it's all gone wrong, we'd better try the other way"? No. The good news that Jesus put into practice during his public career and that he enacted as he went to his death is this: love, faced with rejection, overcomes it with yet more love. "Having loved his own," says Saint John of Jesus on the night he gathered his friends together for one last meal, "he loved them right through to the end."

With that love, revealed in that way, we begin to see what was going on in Jesus's public career. He healed people suffering from all kinds of diseases and ailments. He fed the hungry in ways nobody could quite figure out at the time. He celebrated the arrival of God's kingdom with people of every type, especially the disreputable. *This was the work of new creation.* This was what God becoming king looked like, up close and personal. There's no point making grand statements or gestures if they don't become real in actual lives. Jesus went about making it real, for an old man here and a young girl there, for a dying slave boy and a hemorrhaging woman. He let the power of creative love flow out of him in all directions; though when the power of love met the love of power—for instance, the rich and respectable who didn't want this new creative energy upsetting their way of running the world—it took the form of confrontation and denunciation.

In particular, when this creative love encountered people who were overwhelmed with the weight of their own moral failings, it came out as *forgiveness*. "My child," he said to one young man whose wrongdoings had apparently reduced him to paralysis, "your sins are forgiven." Anyone who has heard that word for themselves knows its creative power. It doesn't just bring you back to the starting line, like someone who has been running up a huge overdraft at the bank and now discovers that the debt has been paid off. Forgiveness somehow puts a whole new deposit into the account—probably because it unlocks the knowledge that you are, after all, a full and fully valued human being, and you no longer need to regard yourself as a hopeless failure. And that news will open *you* up in a whole new way, to become the person God wanted you to become all along. The free gift of forgiveness reveals a new world and invites you to make it your own. That, of course, is one key element in the good news.

Jesus's public career, then, was aimed not only at *announcing* the good news that God was becoming king but at *embodying* it. This is what he said in answer to his poor cousin John: "Look, the blind are receiving their sight, the deaf can hear again, the lame are walking"; in other words, draw your own conclusions. These are the signs that God is on the move, the God of creation and of new creation, the God spoken of in the ancient prophecies, which said that these things would come to pass. And that is why he told all those strange stories—parables, as we call them—which were mostly designed to say, *yes,* God's kingdom is indeed arriving, but *no,* it doesn't look like you thought it would; it looks like *this* instead. It looks like a farmer sowing seeds that result in a lot apparently going to waste but some producing a bumper crop. It looks like a tiny seed that will grow into an astonishingly large bush. It looks like a father with two sons . . . and so on.

Many of these stories were slightly familiar. They would have reminded Jesus's hearers of stories and images from their scriptures. But what he was doing with them was new. New in the same way that his vision of God's kingdom was new. New because *newness* was what he was about. New exodus. New creation. New life, new hope. A new sense of the power and love of the one true God. Good *news.*

But newness came at a price. Jesus himself saw that his good news would be *bad* news to people who had invested heavily in the old ways. Plenty of people looked at him and said he was crazy. Plenty more said he was dangerous. Some said he was in league with the devil. Even his own relatives were shaking their heads in the background. Jesus saw this opposition, this suspicion and hostility, as part of the deal. He had come to set people free, and like Moses with Pharaoh, the king of Egypt, he was confronting the powers that held people captive. He saw himself fighting a strange sort of battle with those powers. He spoke at one point of winning an initial victory that allowed him to make serious inroads into enemy territory, setting people free from many kinds of ailments. He spoke later of the enemy, "the power of darkness," as having a particular time, a "moment" of opportunity (Luke 22:53). That moment was when he was about to be arrested, less than twenty-four hours before his death.

Somehow the creative and recreative love of which he spoke had to do its work by taking all the anticreation forces in the world, all the forces of hatred and fear and decay and death, and exhausting their power by absorbing it into him. This is the point at which the good news was focused for Jesus, the point at which it was also focused for the early church. This is the point at which, as generations will testify, it remains focused for those who announce it today. The good news of Jesus comes to a head in the utterly, catastrophically, appallingly *bad* news of his death.

Have We Really Met the True God?

How can we put all this together? As we look back across the centuries, we notice a recurring theme when people stop for a moment and ask themselves the big questions. Who are we? Where are we? What are we here for—other than to feed, fight, and reproduce? What's wrong? What's the solution? And . . . does the persistent rumor of God, or the gods, or something like that, refer to anything real, or is it just a silly, outdated idea that as a species we can't quite shake off?

I said in chapter 2 that when the apostle Paul announced the good news in northern Greece, it was clearly good news about *God*—about a living and true God as opposed to the many false gods displayed on every street corner in the ancient world. We have seen, throughout this book, that the historic Christian faith is built on the belief that there is such a God, that he is the creator of the universe, that he remains both radically other than the world and intimately involved with it, and that he has been made known, decisively and spectacularly, in and through Jesus of

Nazareth, Israel's Messiah, particularly in his crucifixion and resurrection. The good news about the *past*—the events concerning
Jesus, through which the world has been transformed—is good
news about this God. The good news about the *future*—that there
will come a time when what was begun with Jesus will be completed, and the whole creation will celebrate the powerful love
and justice of God—is good news about this God. The good news
about the *present*—the fact that healing and transformation can
and do happen in the world and in individual human beings—is
good news about this God. What can be said, in conclusion, about
the word *God* and its checkered career through the centuries and
in our own day?

The recurring theme, as we have seen, goes like this. A vague
awareness of forces beyond human control leads to speculation
about divine beings who appear dangerous, quite possibly bad
tempered, and liable to do unpleasant things to human beings unless they are somehow pacified. Sometimes people with the leisure
and the inclination to think such matters through—philosophers,
in other words—consider this and come to different conclusions.
Either there is a divine force within everything and everyone or
the gods are a long way off and not involved at all in our world.
Or perhaps we just can't know. Perhaps there just isn't enough
evidence. One way or another, these moves were designed to
defuse the explosive sense of big bullies in the sky who are out to
get you. All theologies, left to themselves, oscillate between these
positions or variations on them.

Except for the God of Israel. Israel's God, YHWH, was always radically different from any of these pictures. Let's work back through
the options.

Not enough evidence? A devout Jew would have an answer
for such a suggestion. This God had revealed himself to Abraham
and his family, especially in the powerful acts of the exodus. He
continued to reveal himself through the prophets and in various

historical events. He had caused his glorious presence to fill the tabernacle in the wilderness and Solomon's Temple in Jerusalem. Yes, there were long years when people wondered if he had abandoned them. But then, just as rumors faded and hope died, a fresh vision appeared. Most Jews in the time of Jesus believed that there was enough evidence. But for them the problem wasn't intellectual ("What can we know about God?"); the problem was about hope. When would this God do what he had promised, coming back in power and glory to save them and set up his kingdom?

Might the gods be a long way off, as others thought? It is true that Israel's ancient scriptures regularly insist that the one true God exists in a different space from ours. Call it heaven if you like, though recognize if you do that this word is a signpost to an unknowable reality rather than a precise and accurate label for a specific place. But at the same time, this God was powerfully and personally present with his people. He was never under their control, but he promised to be with them, and again and again there were clear signs that he meant what he said. In particular, he promised to come in person to live in their midst. That was what the Temple was all about. It was the place where heaven and earth met. That is something ordinary street-level pagans of the ancient world, without much philosophical training, might have understood. They too had temples that were supposed to be where the god or goddess met with worshippers. But when Israel's God showed up, there was something quite different, as we will see in a moment.

Might the world simply be suffused with a kind of divine presence and power, as many believed in Paul's day? The ancient Israelites certainly celebrated the goodness of the present world. Not for them the mealymouthed rejection of the material universe embraced by some dualistic philosophies. Some of their great poems imagined all of creation singing God's praises. But this already shows that for them goodness was always a *gift* from beyond. Their God remained the creator, the one who had made the world, not simply a divine presence within the world. He was indeed present, especially with those who needed him most—the poor and the oppressed, for a start. But it was the presence of one who remained, at the same time, completely outside the creation, as the writer of a novel may be felt as a personal presence in the story and yet remains completely outside the book.

So might the cheerful old pagan stories have a grain of truth? All those gods and goddesses living on Mount Olympus, squabbling, plotting, generally behaving like a dysfunctional royal court, but also intervening, appearing and disappearing, helping some humans in their projects and frustrating others—were there actually divine powers like that at work in the world? It does indeed look as though Israel's God was *alive* in the same way as those divinities were thought to be. To the horror of philosophically minded folk in the ancient and modern worlds, Israel's God makes plans and carries them out; he makes promises and doesn't forget them; he is passionately and compassionately involved with his people, with the world, and especially with the poor and needy. He is, in short, an untidy god. Philosophy tidies things up; Israel's God blows his fresh wind and scatters things about the room that humans had just sorted out. He is not, in other words, imprisoned in any human system. He is not merely a god. He is God.

I hope this makes it clear that today's questions about God are basically the same questions that people have faced through the years. The philosophers tried various ways of putting the wild old pagan rumors to rest, partly to assure people that they didn't need to be afraid after all. The God of Israel is constantly telling people, "Don't be afraid," but for a very different reason: not because he isn't interested, not because he is simply the sum total of all natural forces, but because he *is* interested and *is* active within the world—but his interest and his activity are those of the wise creator who loves his creation and is determined to put it right in the end. He is the God of good news.

Now put all this into the time of the early Christians. Everything we have said about Israel's God comes into sudden and shocking focus with Jesus. His first followers quickly came to the conclusion that *the God of Israel had come at last in person, as he had promised, to rescue his people and establish his rule in the world.* Jesus was, as it were, the new temple. He was the place where heaven and earth met. This was what it looked like when the true God came in power and love to rescue the poor and needy and bring the forgiveness of sins. The early Christian good news was good news about God *because it was good news about Jesus.*

That is the hidden truth inside the story we have been telling throughout this book. The philosophers were right to reject the old myths about the ordinary pagan divinities. But what they offered instead, while interesting in itself, didn't go nearly far enough. The news that ran around the world with the message about Jesus was that there *was* a genuine God, that he was the creator of all, and that he had fulfilled his ancient promises in dealing with evil at the root and launching his project of new creation.

That message was powerful—in two senses. First, it carried *intellectual conviction.* It made a lot of sense, once people got over the initial shock of its big claims (first, that the Jews were right all along; second, that God raised Jesus from the dead). Second, it carried *spiritual power,* the power to transform lives, to heal bodies, to reconcile enemies, to generate and sustain a new sort of family life in which all were welcome. Paul, writing to the Corinthians and looking back on the beginning of his work among them, said he was determined that their faith should rest not on human wisdom but on God's power. He didn't try to fit his message into their clever categories, to offer them something they could accept and feel proud of having understood within their own world. He

allowed the power of the good news to work, healing and transforming lives. Do that and the challenge to intellectual conviction comes naturally in its wake.

Now bring all this forward to the fifteenth and sixteenth
centuries. The old pagan gods had crept back into popular
imagination—except that they were painted in Christian colors.
People again lived in fear of a vengeful deity who might strike
them with lightning in the present or hurl them into hell after
their deaths. In the late Middle Ages, though everyone gave lip
service to mainstream religious belief, it doesn't seem to have
made a radical difference in most people's lives. But then two
things happened. First, some writers picked up once more the ancient split-world philosophy. Perhaps, they suggested, God and the
world were after all separated by a great gulf. Perhaps the world
was simply going on its way under its own steam, its own internal
impulses. That was one philosophical answer to the problem of
a dangerous, perhaps angry God. Second, the sixteenth-century
Reformers announced that the Bible, when properly read, offered
a radically different picture. The living God had acted to save the
world through Jesus, especially through his death.

Philosophy and Christian reform: two answers to the same
question. What are we to do about this distant, vengeful God?
Answer 1: Such a being doesn't exist. If there is a god, he's a long
way away. Nothing to worry about. Answer 2: It's all right, because Jesus has died in our place. He has taken our punishment.
Believe in him and you'll be saved.

Because the leading Reformers were nothing if not teachers of
the Bible, they went much farther than this. They saw, in many
wonderful ways, that the essentially pagan picture of a vengeful
God was quite wrong. They insisted on a fully trinitarian vision of salvation: it wasn't that a kind, gentle, suffering Jesus was
rescuing us from his vicious and angry father, but that the father
himself was utterly loving, giving his own son, his own second

self, to rescue us from the plight into which we had fallen. One cannot read the major Reformers and not be struck by this theme of divine love, and by the joy and hope it produces.

But at the popular level the old picture persisted. That, I think, is what has continued to drive popular presentations to this day. It takes intellectual and spiritual effort to maintain one's grip on the full biblical revelation of the love and justice of God. It is much easier to speak in the old language of the angry God and the merciful Jesus. And even when preachers and teachers have done their best, people still get the wrong idea. They try to fit together bits and pieces of what they hear from the pulpit into a different frame of reference . . . and so the old pagan ideas come back once more, at least in what people hear.

That, I think, is the root cause of the new atheisms of the last generation, whether it be the angry and militant atheism of Richard Dawkins and his ilk or the softer, more wistful atheism of someone like the novelist Julian Barnes ("I don't believe in God, but I miss him"). Many people, picking up strands from some elements of Christian speaking and writing, find it difficult to distinguish the message from violent quasi-pagan notions. Others, perhaps, even reading a book like the present one, may think, as a recent correspondent put it to me, that it seems as though we are being asked to believe in a tribal god, the god of one particular first-century Middle Eastern people. Faced with that, it might seem wiser to go with the god of the philosophers, perhaps with the addition that this being is actually a god of love. (That's a hard trick to pull off, but you can see why people might want to try.)

But as Blaise Pascal said in the seventeenth century, when you get to know the God of Abraham, Isaac, and Jacob, you realize that he is quite different from the god of the philosophers. And as we might add, when you see that this true God is fully and finally revealed in and through Jesus of Nazareth, you realize that this constitutes good news indeed—good news for all people, including even the philosophers but perhaps especially those who for years have labored under the delusion that Christianity is just like ancient paganism but with a particularly nasty bit in the middle.

All these ideas swirl to and fro in popular culture today. Many people who had a strong dose of one kind of Christianity in their youth and were thoroughly put off by it (or by what they understood of it) have continued to reject the Christian tradition in later life. One can understand why. Nor do I imagine that the present book will necessarily resolve all the problems that such people have, or that it will necessarily enable Christian preachers and teachers to present a less misleading version in the future. But I hope I have said enough to demonstrate that the caricatures are simply caricatures and that the God who the early Christians believed had revealed himself in Jesus—and in the Spirit of Jesus, now at work through the good news in the world, in the hearts and minds of men, women, and children all over the place—is the one true God, who calls to them with sovereign love and summons them to join in his work of new creation. And that this was, and still is, good news.

I do not say that it is easy to believe in this God. It is not. I once saw a book with the title *The God I Want,* and I shuddered. Such a god must be an idol. If we ever get to the point where we say, "There! There's a God you can believe in!" we will know at once that we have fitted the idea of God into a preexisting gap in our minds. The true God—if there is such a one—cannot be an object in our world. *We* are objects in *his* world. In the same way, he cannot sit comfortably as an idea in our minds. *We* are, in that sense, ideas in *his* mind. That is why Paul twice corrects himself: "Now that you have come to know God," he begins, and then says, "or, better, to be known *by* God" (see Gal. 4:9). His point is that the good news comes knocking on doors that we didn't even know we had; it flings open the curtains on windows we didn't know existed to reveal the rising sun flooding the room with glory when we had imagined that all light came from candles; it woos our cold hearts and awakens them, like someone falling in love for the first time, to a joy and fulfillment never before imagined.

No doubt there is more, much more, to be said. This book is just a beginning. But the point is this: the good news of which Christians speak is indeed good news. Once you understand it and are grasped by this, it is the best news you could ever hear. To pay attention to it—to look carefully at the news about the past (what happened in Jesus) and about the future (the eventual new creation), and to begin to discover the news about the present (the present challenge of God's kingdom in the world, and of the transformation of your own life within that)—is to see the world with different eyes. To see God with different eyes. To see your neighbor with different eyes. To see yourself with different eyes. This is the challenge of the good news for today and tomorrow.

8

Praying the Good News

WHEN JESUS WENT about telling people the good news, he gave them a prayer to pray. The word *gospel,* meaning "good news," doesn't feature explicitly in this prayer. But what the prayer does instead is to give us an important way of getting inside the good news—or perhaps we should say, letting the good news get inside *us.* I said earlier that our calling is not simply to believe the good news. It is to become good-news people. And we can't do this by simply trying hard. We can only do it through prayer. And if Jesus himself was and is the ultimate good-news person, then the prayer he gave his followers is the best possible place to start.

But here we come to a puzzle. The prayer we call the Lord's Prayer (Matt. 6:9–13) is rightly famous. Many people, even if they never go near a church, can still recite it, having learned it when they were young. But there's a strange thing about the Lord's Prayer. In fact, several strange things. If we were to start with most people's vision of the good news and turn it into a prayer, it probably wouldn't come out like the prayer Jesus taught. Instead, we might get prayers like this:

> *O God, please forgive me my sins and take me to heaven forever (and, by the way, help me to stop sinning now).*
> *O God, thank you for showing me how to live. Please help me to do it.*
> *O God, please give me enough food so I can at least feed my family.*
> *O God, please bring justice to your world, which needs it so badly.*
> *O God, please heal Annie, Ben, Caroline, David, Eleanor, and Frank (and so on right through the alphabet).*

Now, none of these prayers is bad in itself. Much, much better to pray for forgiveness, for moral vision and courage, for food, for justice, and for healing than not to do so. But the Lord's Prayer doesn't start off with any of these, though they can all be included.

I have a sense that the Lord's Prayer is not just a list of key topics. It is a list of priorities. Most of us, I suspect, start our praying near the end and may never really get back to the beginning. Perhaps one way to learn about the good news and to become good-news people is to learn to pray this prayer in the order Jesus taught it. That is harder than it might seem.

Think of it like this. The Lord's Prayer invites us to come inside, as though we were entering a great and splendid mansion, and to make ourselves at home. But most of us, I think, come into this building through the wrong entrance.

Imagine you have been invited to a wonderful house. You drive up a long driveway toward the main building, but having parked your car, you lose your way and find yourself going in through a door around the back. You creep inside and begin to look around. You find yourself in a small outer kitchen; there is some food being prepared and several garbage bins. This is not what you expected, though the sight of the food makes you hungry. Then you find your way slowly through to the real kitchen, where a full meal is almost ready. This looks good, but you know it wasn't the right way to enter. So you continue to explore the house and find yourself at last in the main entrance hall. Now you start to see how the whole house works. Finally, you come to the front door—and there, with his back to you, is your host. He has been watching out for you. When you greet him, he is puzzled that you seem to have come in the wrong way but delighted you're here at last. Now you can sit down and enjoy his company. And yes, it will very soon be time for the wonderful meal.

Of course, as long as you get inside the house, that's the main thing, even if you break in by a window. But once you're in—and once you find you are a welcome guest, not an intruder—then it's worthwhile trying to figure out how the house actually works and what it might be like to come in properly, by the front door.

But let's start where we are, with the things mentioned right at the end of the prayer. Because most of us, as I say, come in at the back door. We begin at the end. (The usual ending, by the way— the phrase about "the kingdom, the power, and the glory"—was an early Christian addition to the prayer. We'll stick with what Jesus said.)

Most of us—most human beings who pray—begin with the most obvious prayer of all.

Help!

Don't bring us into the great trial,
But rescue us from evil.

Old soldiers sometimes say, "There are no atheists in foxholes." (A foxhole, in military slang, is a shallow pit in a dangerous place on the battlefield.) That may or may not be true. But it is undoubtedly true that many people who don't normally pray will, in times of great stress, say some sort of prayer. And like Jesus's disciples on the boat in the storm, most of us in those circumstances don't have the time for leisured reflection on what prayer is or what form it should take. All we can do is cry out, "Help!"

If we had the time, we might say something like, "If there's bad stuff out there, rescue me from it!" or "Bad things are about to happen, so please stop them!" Or if we wanted to put it in more formal language, we might say, "Deliver us from evil!"

This is what I mean by saying that most of us come into the Lord's Prayer by the back door. That's fine—if you're in, you're in. But might it be perhaps a good thing to work toward the front door? Perhaps even eventually to figure out what might happen if we began there instead?

If you asked someone at the "Help!" stage of praying what the good news might be, they would probably say, "The only good news I'm interested in is getting out of this mess!" That's perfectly all right. That is how people often begin. But it's not a great place to stop.

The second thing we might pray is also a squeal for help, but it's a bit more focused. It's what people tend to pray when they find themselves in a difficult or stressful situation: "Why are you doing this to me?"

This is what we say to God when the key snaps in the car door and it's ten degrees below and we're in the wrong part of town. It's what we say when, for the third time that week, the hole in the roof we thought had been mended starts to leak. It's what we say when a child (or a parent) does something that drives us mad. It's what we say when the work colleague with anger-management problems lets fly at us yet one more time. At least, it's what some people say on such occasions. There is a sense that God may somehow be responsible, and that perhaps, just perhaps, this is some kind of test . . . and that we may be in danger of failing it.

The grown-up version of this prayer looks like this: "Lead us not into temptation!" In other words, "Don't make me face this kind of test!" The word *temptation* is associated in our minds with pressure, from inside or outside, to do something we know to be wrong. In biblical terms, that is one type of testing, where we find ourselves put under stress, like a steel bar being checked to see if it will stand the strain when installed in the relevant machine. There are also many other kinds of testing: things that, as we say, try our patience, our courage, our faith, hope, or love.

The prayer "Lead us not into temptation," or (as it's sometimes translated today) "Do not bring us to the time of trial," sounds much calmer than this. Fair enough; it's good to pray this prayer in advance of the moment when you find yourself squealing it out. But in essence it's the same thing. "How can you do this to me? What are you trying to prove? Why am I having to face this stuff? *Don't put me in the position where I might crack under pressure!*"

People at this stage of praying, like those at the "Help!" stage, are looking for one kind of good news. They want the pressure to stop—or perhaps for it not to start in the first place. That will be good news enough: a period of respite. A chance to regroup, to restore balance and morale. That is no bad thing. This—to continue the illustration—really is an important room in the house.

But "Help!"—or rather, God's response to this prayer—is not the whole of the good news. Not by any stretch of the imagination.

That is the point where many Christians move backward in the prayer to the next major petition.

Forgive Us

And forgive us the things we owe,
As we too have forgiven what was owed to us.

Or in the usual language, "Forgive us our trespasses, as we forgive those who trespass against us." Actually, many Christians conveniently forget the second half, partly because it's so difficult and partly because it is such a remarkable thing that we include in a prayer this one moral commitment on our part. (This is reflected in Jesus's own teaching, as for instance in Matt. 18.)

For many Christians, this simply *is* the good news: that though we are sinners, God has dealt with our sin so that we can now be forgiven. Often, as we know, this is coupled with *present spirituality* and *future hope*. If my sins are forgiven, I can be at peace with God and enjoy his presence right now; if my sins are forgiven, I won't go to hell after all. Once more, let's say it: for many Christians, *this simply is the good news*. Not a dogma more, not a dogma less.

And yes, of course it is part of the good news. Yes, the Lord's Prayer, here as elsewhere, subtly reflects the larger ministry of Jesus. At this point particularly, it reflects his assurance of forgiveness to many people during his ministry and above all "giving his life as a ransom for many" at the end. This is all enormously important. Anyone who imagines he or she has a handle on the gospel but somehow forgets the forgiveness of sins has got hold of the wrong gospel.

But this isn't the whole of the Lord's Prayer. It isn't even in the first half. And that is because it isn't the whole of the good news. It's a key part but not the whole thing. *Not even the main thing.* It is indeed a room in the house, but we are still working our way in from the back kitchen. We haven't even got near the entrance hall yet.

At this point many Christians work back in the prayer to the point where, as well as asking to be rescued, to be spared the present trial, and to be forgiven, they realize they need to ask for all sorts of other things.

Daily Bread

Give us today the bread we need now.

Or in the traditional language, "Give us this day our daily bread." Bread here is important in its own right. Unless we eat fairly regularly, nothing much is going to happen. But it also stands here as a symbol for all the other things we want to request. Forget the caricature ("O Lord, won't you buy me a Mercedes-Benz?"). Asking for what we need is appropriate. It's what children do with parents. That is precisely the relationship God wants us to have with him.

This aspect of the good news, too, is firmly rooted in the ministry of Jesus. Continuing the story of coming through the house the wrong way, this is the dining room. There really is a meal being set out, and we really are welcome, even if we've come through the back passage rather than through the front door. Jesus fed hungry people. This was part of the good news, an enacted symbol of the coming kingdom in which everyone would be given what they needed. I hope it's starting to become clear: what Jesus was *saying* about good news was linked at every point with what he was *doing* to embody it. This isn't because his deeds were, so to speak, visual aids of the real thing, which was his teaching of great truths. It is because the great truths he was teaching were precisely about the creator God coming to renew and restore creation! That *was* the great thing, the real thing.

Jesus's feeding of hungry people links closely with the celebrations he participated in—dining and feasting with all sorts of people who were thrilled to bits to think that God's kingdom was coming at last and excited beyond measure to think that they were in on the start of it all. And as we know, these meals all led to one last meal—the Last Supper, as we call it—which was also a celebration but of a very different kind. Jesus made it clear that this was a kingdom-meal but that the coming of the kingdom would be accomplished through his own death. Somehow, "Give us today our daily bread" points on to a larger reality about which Jesus spoke on various occasions: that somehow his own life and death would themselves become the transformative food that would enable people to live as new-creation people.

This prayer for daily bread, when we take it seriously in the context of Jesus's public career, as well as his death and resurrection, doesn't just mean, "Give us what we need right now." It includes that, but it stops that prayer from being merely selfish or pragmatic. It insists that what we need right now (and, indeed, what we *think* we need right now!) has to be held within the larger context of Jesus's entire kingdom program, as well as his death and resurrection.

This means that we shouldn't highlight this aspect of the good news in such a way as to forget the others. We will come to the larger kingdom issues presently. For the moment, though, we note that some people might be inclined to highlight God's desire to meet people's physical needs to the exclusion of other elements. If the good news means feeding the hungry people in the world (and housing the homeless and helping the weakest and most vulnerable people in society), they might think, then that's fine! Bring it on! (But by implication, don't bother us with all that pious stuff about forgiveness and temptation and so on.) This can be, for some, a way of getting off the hook. "Let's just do the practical bit and don't bother about spirituality." But the whole prayer resists that. Every bit needs every other bit. Every bit of the good news needs every other bit. We can't just stay in the dining room without completing our journey through the house to the front door, where we should have started in the first place.

So far, then, working backward, we have a prayer for help, a prayer to not be tested to the breaking point, a prayer for forgiveness, and a prayer for bread. That's fine. All these are important, even if people too often approach this great house through the back door. What happens next? What happens when we come through from the kitchen and dining room into the main entrance hall?

Here and Now

May your kingdom come,
May your will be done
As in heaven, so on earth.

The traditional words go so well with everything Jesus did and said—everything Jesus *was*—that simply to repeat them appears to sum up his whole agenda. "Your kingdom come! Your will be done, on earth as in heaven!" And with this, we sense—if we have our wits about us—that we have turned a corner. Up to this point, working back through the prayer, we have focused on our own needs. Now we look up and see a larger plan. *It's time for God to become king—here and now.* Now at last we come into the entrance hall and glimpse our host for the first time.

Granted, the theme of God's kingdom was also often seen by people in Jesus's day as being specifically about their own needs. Many Jews of Jesus's time, as we have seen, spoke of God becoming king to refer to social and political liberation from Rome, establishment of a free and independent Jewish state, and peace and prosperity for all God's people. Some might even have envisaged the pagan nations coming to learn about this remarkable, unique God; this was important in some biblical prophecies. Thus many Jews of Jesus's day had, as it were, their own meaning for "give us bread" (we want peace and prosperity), "forgive us our sins" (whatever we did to deserve this mess, please wipe it out), "don't test us to breaking point" (if things go on this way, we're all doomed), and "help!" (we're in a mess—do something!). When they heard people talking about God's kingdom, they had various natural ways of understanding this, mainly in terms of the later petitions in the prayer. We often find ourselves doing the same if we're not careful.

God's kingdom does indeed address all these issues. But the way Jesus announced God's kingdom—and the way he both *enacted* and *explained* it—meant that he was telling people to look up, beyond their concerns, beyond the way they thought everything ought to work out. This is why his good news both was and wasn't what people expected or hoped for. That's the same for us, too. That is why Jesus told his followers that if they wanted to continue in his company, they had to "take up their cross and follow him," and that only those who were prepared to lose their lives would actually save them.

The challenge of the kingdom, as Jesus presented it (and as he lived and died for it), is the challenge of seeing that the living God, when he becomes king, has plans for his people and for the world that will translate all our hopes, longings, and desires to another plane entirely.

The danger at this point is that people who hear this message might think, "There! I knew it! It wasn't about bread and freedom after all. It was all something spiritual. That's not going to help me here and now." This would be a radical misunderstanding, and one of the most important phrases in the whole prayer explains why: "Your kingdom come, your will be done, *on earth as in heaven*."

I am regularly astonished at how many Christians in the Western world who say that prayer again and again ignore the plain meaning of the words. "On earth as in heaven." Not "in heaven as in heaven"—a prayer for God to take us to heaven at last or give us a heavenly spiritual experience here and now—but "on *earth* as in heaven." We cannot stress too strongly, or too often, that the whole message of the New Testament—the whole point of the mission and message of Jesus, of his life, death, and resurrection—is the *coming together of heaven and earth*, not their separation.

Look at it like this. God made heaven and earth to be complementary. It is his clearly stated will, as various New Testament writers insist, that they should be joined together in the end within the eventual new creation. *The whole point of what Jesus was doing was that this coming together of earth and heaven was starting right then, with his work.* That union was to be hugely costly, of course, because of the mess earth was in: hence the cross and resurrection. And the point of the story, the way the four Gospels tell it, was that this coming together of earth and heaven was decisively launched precisely through these cataclysmic events.

This may sound exciting, and it is. But it is also deeply challenging. And here's the point. If we approach the Lord's Prayer backward, as we have been doing—and as, I have been suggesting, many Christians do, at least by implication—then we are bound to make the mistake of reducing God's kingdom to God doing what we want him to do. That, of course, is to turn God into an idol, a tame puppet that we invoke to get our own way. *And the whole point of the Lord's Prayer, at the heart of Jesus's good news, is to see everything the other way around.*

But at least, working backward to the start of the prayer, if we can make the step from "help" to "forgive" to "feed," and then to "kingdom," there is a chance that our priorities may get sorted out. Better to start by praying for God's kingdom, and then let God himself reshape what that means, than not to pray it at all.

But better still, of course, is to turn our gaze to God himself—to God as we see him revealed in Jesus—and to quieten our over-eager, fussy, look-at-me prayers and start focusing on God. What would it *really* look like if God were to become king? It's time to come through the house and, however shamefacedly, greet our host at last.

Once we find ourselves addressing that question and doing so with the full biblical story in the background and Jesus in the foreground, then we will begin at last to understand more fully what the good news really is. The good news is that *the living God is indeed establishing his kingdom on earth as in heaven, through the fin-ished work of Jesus, and is inviting people of all sorts to share not only in the benefits of this kingdom but also in the work through which it will come to its ultimate completion.* To grasp that good news fully, or rather to be grasped by it, will mean being turned inside out by it, so that our self-centered prayers (for help, for rescue, for forgiveness, and for bread) will turn into the God-centered prayer for God's kingdom to come in God's way. Let's put it this way, turning the illustration around for a moment. Suppose it's your house and you're inviting God into it. But when you do that, you find that God isn't just a polite guest who sits on the edge of his chair and takes care not to spill crumbs on the carpet. When God comes into the house, he comes as the rightful owner. He may well start rearranging the furniture.

Come back to the original picture. Here we are, guests in God's house, coming by mistake through the back door. But now we are in the entrance hall. Once we take our courage in both hands and decide to move back through the Lord's Prayer to pray for God's kingdom to come on earth as in heaven, we might be ready to approach the front door at last and greet our host, who has been standing there waiting for us. This brings us to what is meant to be the first petition in the prayer:

Honor and Glory to Your Name!

May your name be honored.

There is no way this prayer can be anything other than God-centered. That, no doubt, is why many of us find it so hard to pray it. It is the ultimate act of worship. It is meant to set the tone for the entire prayer. It is, in fact, the very heart of the good news. *God's name is hallowed, honored, glorified.* "Hallowed be your name."

Sometimes, when we say the word *hallowed* in ordinary speech, we simply mean "respected" or even "historic" (as when people talk grandly about the "hallowed halls" of a university or college). Hallowing God's name certainly includes respect. But the good news is that God isn't just a being whose name we should respect, though of course we should do that. God is the father, the stunningly generous creator, the supremely wise ruler and guide of the nations. He is the father of Jesus. He is the God who makes promises and keeps them. He is the lord of the angels. He is utterly faithful, utterly loving, utterly determined to bring heaven and earth together in a glorious and fruitful marriage.

In the great vision of the book of Revelation, all creatures in heaven and earth worship him, adore him, and celebrate his goodness, his power, and his love. The challenge for human beings is to sum up that praise, to turn it into articulate speech, to discover more and more fully *why* God is to be praised and to say so. This opening petition in the Lord's Prayer aims to do just that. The starting point for all fully Christian prayer is *worship*. You could put that the other way around: learning to worship—the word means "celebrating the worth" of someone or something, in this case God himself—is learning to be a Christian.

This prayer thus aims to celebrate the summit of the good news.

The good news isn't primarily about us receiving help when we need it (though that's included), rescue when we're under intense pressure (though that comes, too), forgiveness (though we need it and will be given it, as long as we, too, become forgiving people), or food for the journey (though that will be provided). It isn't primarily even about God's kingdom coming and his will being done on earth as in heaven, though that remains central. *The good news is primarily that God—the generous God, the loving God—is being honored, will be honored, has been utterly and supremely honored, in the life, death, and resurrection of Jesus.* That is why, when Jesus was facing the fact that his hour had come to suffer and die, he wondered whether he should really say, "Father, save me from this moment" (a bit like "Don't let us be tested to breaking point"). He didn't. Instead, he settled on praying, "Father, glorify your name!" (John 12:27–28). And the Father did.

Indeed, one of the central points of John's Gospel in particular is that Jesus's entire public career, and particularly his death, served as a display, in action, of the glory of God. As we may recall, the ancient prophecies about good news focused exactly on this point. The messenger who was telling good news to God's people was to declare that "the glory of the LORD shall be revealed, and all people shall see it together" (Isa. 40:5). The whole of the Lord's Prayer, with this petition as its launching point, is there so that Jesus's followers, during his own lifetime and on into the life of the church, can celebrate this revelation-in-action of the divine glory and learn more and more fully the meaning of the divine name. The Hebrew word that, in the ancient scriptures, is the proper name of Israel's God is YHWH, which is hard to translate but includes the ideas "I AM," "I AM WHO I AM," and consequently "I WILL BE WHO I WILL BE" (see Exod. 3:13–15). He is the sovereign one, the glorious, generous creator. He is the source of all delight, all daylight, all that is lovely, lively, and liberating. This is the ultimate good news. *This God has come to be with us, to celebrate his name and his nature, to make all things new.*

And now, perhaps, we are ready for the opening words of the prayer.

Heavenly Father

Our father in heaven . . .

Now at last we are meeting our host. He doesn't mind that we came in through the back door by mistake. He's glad we are here now and is welcoming us warmly. And when we learn to call him Father—however difficult that may be for some people, for good reason—we are not simply reflecting a timeless truth that Jesus came to teach. Jesus was announcing a new reality breaking in upon a surprised and unready world—that there was one true God, whom Israel had sometimes in the past called Father, and that in and through Jesus this fatherhood could and should become a reality for everybody. "To all who received him," wrote John in his Gospel, "to all who believed in his name, to them he gave the right to be called 'children of God.'" The idea of God as father, known fleetingly in Israel and very occasionally among the non-Jewish peoples, had exploded into the world in a new way. Jesus was making it real. That is the good news.

Another problem. A century or so ago, some teachers tried to summarize the Christian message by talking about "the Fatherhood of God and the Brotherhood of Man." This grand-sounding phrase—even when we try to make its language more gender-inclusive, as we do now—rings hollow today, partly because some of those who made it their slogan were among those who were most enthusiastic about fighting the First World War. The idea that all people are brothers or siblings took a huge battering in that war, and though people still try to reaffirm it, there is a sense that, like scorched children, we don't want to go near the fire a second time.

The problem was precisely that such teachers were translating the unique *announcement* of Jesus—the good *news*—into a fine-sounding *ideal,* that is, into good *advice* yet again. They didn't really want Jesus to have been the point around which world history pivots. A moral example, perhaps; a great teacher of timeless truths, certainly—but not the turning point of the world.

But you can't pull things apart like that. Jesus was not teaching a timeless truth that might in principle have been articulated at any time or place. He wasn't holding up an ideal and saying, "Let's all see if we can live up to this!" He was announcing a new reality breaking in upon a surprised and unready world. And in this prayer, he was inviting his followers to explore this new reality and make it their own.

Becoming Good-News People

So what happens when we pray the prayer the right way around? *We become good-news people.* That is true, actually, whenever you pray, because prayer means standing between the one true God and his world, becoming a place where the love of this God and the life of this world (and especially the pain of this world) are somehow held together. That can be costly. There is a great depth of spiritual meaning to be explored at that point, though not here.

But the truth of becoming good-news people becomes supremely clear when you pray *this* prayer and allow its full dynamic to work out both in how you pray and in how you then live. We mustn't fool ourselves. This prayer isn't just a string of miscellaneous requests. As we've seen in working backward through the prayer, following the route many people actually take in their spiritual growth, there is a fascinating sequence here. When we turn around and go through it the proper way, every petition creates a context for the next one. When we call God Father, we know in the next line that praying for his name to be hallowed won't be a matter of a thundering, bullying god giving himself airs while we cower in a corner. Likewise, when we truly pray for God's kingdom to come on earth as in heaven, we can then move on to pray for bread, forgiveness, and help without the risk that those prayers will collapse into mere selfish or pragmatic petitions. (There is nothing wrong with bringing our own heartfelt needs, hopes, and desires to God. We are constantly encouraged to do that. The thing that can go wrong is to imagine that we can twist God's kingdom into the shape of our muddled and often misguided longings.)

Praying this prayer, then, and praying it in the right order allow us not only to *know* and *believe* the good news but to become part of it ourselves. This takes us right back to that point in the story where we reminded ourselves that God made human beings in the first place *to reflect his image into the world*. God wants to run his world, to bring his love and wisdom and purposes to bear on the world, *through* human beings. The foundation of the good news is that through Jesus—the ultimate human being, the true image bearer—the living God has done this once and for all. It has been done. It doesn't need to be done again. The world is a different place because of Jesus.

But when people believe this and find their own lives *transformed* by that belief, they are in turn recruited to be part of the continuing image-bearing work. They become transformed people who are then transforming the world. They become healed people through whom God brings healing to the world. They are put right with God ("justified"), so that they can be putting-right people for the world ("justice"). They are people whose lives have been transformed by the good news of Jesus so that they can be good-news people for the world. This is why Jesus pronounced God's blessing on them—the hungry-for-justice people, the merciful, the meek, the peacemakers, and so on. And this is why the Sermon on the Mount, which begins with that list almost as a recruiting call for people to sign on as kingdom-people, comes to its focus in this prayer. In the Lord's Prayer. In the prayer that makes us utterly humble before God and utterly human in reflecting him into his world.

That, you see, is what prayer does, and that's why a focus on prayer is so important as we round off this introduction to the good news. All prayer stands with arms outstretched, one to embrace the loving God, the other to embrace the needy world. As we take up that stand—whether literally or simply in our hearts!—we find that our own prayers, our own hopes and needs and longings and fears, are somehow contained within it. The call to God as Father includes it all, though it goes beyond it all. The prayer for God to glorify his own name includes it all, though, like Jesus's own prayer, it opens the door for God to do, whether without us or through us and in us—whatever is good in his sight. The prayer for God's kingdom to come on earth as in heaven is the prayer *both* for Jesus's own lifetime—when it was answered gloriously in his death and resurrection—*and* for our own day, when it will be answered yet more gloriously in the ultimate "new heaven and new earth" of Revelation 21 and 22 and the "liberated creation" of Romans 8. And once we have got God's fatherhood, his name, and his kingdom in the right perspective, everything else follows. There will then be plenty of room for the other prayers we will always need and want to pray, for food (for the world and for ourselves), for forgiveness, for release from unbearable pressure, for help.

This prayer, then, not only looks back to Jesus as the one through whom the world became a different place—as the one whose life, death, and resurrection are, forever, the good news.

It also helps us to live, in our own day and our own very different circumstances, as good-news people, people who have been grasped by that good news, people through whom the good news can extend in love and mercy into all the world. That must always begin with prayer. It won't end there; often the answer to our prayer will begin, "Well, you could start by doing *this* or *that*." That's as it should be. Prayer is part of the larger vocation in which we humans are supposed to be bringing God's love to bear on his world. But if it doesn't start with prayer—with a prayer shaped the way the Lord's Prayer is shaped—it may well end up being simply a version of our own agendas, which we hope God will validate retrospectively. And the answer to that is: he may, but he may not. All kingdom work, all good-news work in the world, remains God's work, even though he shares quite a bit of it with us. It is vital that we remind ourselves of that day by day. And the best way of doing that is through the good-news prayer—the prayer Jesus taught us.

All Christian prayer, then, and supremely the Lord's Prayer, enables us to be fully at home in God's house, whichever door we come in by. But we don't come in simply to rest and be refreshed. We enter in order to learn and share God's plans and purposes. Prayer is one way we do both these things. Only with prayer at the center will the work of the kingdom go forward. Once we are grasped by the good news, we must learn to be shaped by the good news. In prayer, we learn to *become* good news.

ACKNOWLEDGMENTS

I am once again very grateful to friends and publishers who have read successive drafts of this book and offered me all kinds of helpful comments. Simon Kingston and Philip Law at SPCK have given me their usual wisdom and advice, and Mickey Maudlin at HarperOne has steered the whole project from the early idea through many periods of trial and error to its present form. I am, of course, responsible for any errors that remain. I am also grateful to many friends around the world who have offered encouragement, advice, and prayer. Among these are David and Karen Seemuth in Wisconsin and Guy and Katie Thomas in Surrey, whose own ministries are launching out in new directions at this time. This book is gratefully dedicated to them.

SCRIPTURE INDEX

SUBJECT INDEX

Explore
other books by
N. T. Wright

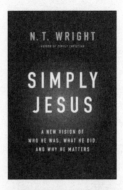

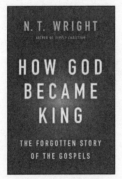

and more . . .